AUSTRALIAN
C U I S I N E

A book containing recipes with a distinctive
Australian style – traditional recipes
and recipes adopted and adapted
from Australia's multicultural society.

AUSTRALIAN
CUISINE

MAUREEN SIMPSON

an
ABC
BOOK

Published by ABC Enterprises for the
AUSTRALIAN BROADCASTING CORPORATION
20 Atchison Street (Box 8888) Crows Nest NSW 2065

First published in 1987 by Methuen Haynes
(an imprint of Methuen Australia Pty Ltd)
This revised paperback edition published 1990

National Library of Australia
Cataloguing-in-Publication entry
Simpson, Maureen, 1933–   .
   Australian cuisine.
   Rev. ed.
   ISBN 0 7333 0074 X.
   1. Cookery. I. Title.
641.5

Photographs by John Garth
Designed by Nuttshell Graphics
Set in Century Oldstyle by Midland Typesetters, Victoria
Printed in Hong Kong by South China Printing Co.

CONTENTS

To dearest Ian,
with all my love

Thanks to Susan Haynes who initially invited
me to write the first edition of *Australian
Cuisine* and home economist Louise Patniotis
who assisted with the careful testing and
double testing of the recipes. This paperback
edition of *Australian Cuisine* is the result of
listeners' interest and requests for recipes from
the book when mentioned on ABC Radio in
'The Weekend' program on 2BL (702). My very
special thanks to 'The Weekend' and in
particular to John Hall, Bob Hughes, Graham
Pearce and Murdo McCleod.

FOREWORD

Australia has come of age . . . and, yes, I do think there is an Australian Cuisine. It's young and imaginative, and although some of our traditional recipes are inherited from the early days, many of the dishes we prepare for our families or choose to eat when dining out are as wide and varied as the land itself.

Unlike the more established countries, we are not governed by hundreds of years of tradition which dictate the 'correct' way to prepare regional dishes.

Australians are by nature innovative, and this is reflected in our cuisine as well. We have adopted dishes from the multicultural society in which we live, and because we don't always have the reverence for hundreds of years of tradition we adapt these recipes to suit our tastes, or more often to use whatever ingredients are on hand. This has resulted in a distinctive Australian style.

In this book I have selected the essence of what I see as an Australian Cuisine. I hope it will be a book that Australians will relate to through the recipes, and visually as well. Photographer, John Garth, whose work was once described to me as 'pure poetry', has captured a distinctly Australian feel to the photographs. John has a certain magic with his photography which some say makes the food look so real you could pick it right off the pages, and I agree. For the Australian flowers used in the photographs, I would like to thank the Wildflower Farm at Somersby, NSW, which kept me supplied with gum tips and our rare and beautiful native flowers.

Maureen Simpson

CONVERSIONS

METRIC CUPS	GRAMS (approx)	OUNCES (approx)
1 cup butter	250	8¾
1 cup biscuit crumbs	110	3¾
1 cup breadcrumbs, soft	60	2
1 cup breadcrumbs, dry	125	4½
1 cup cheese, grated	125	4½
1 cup cocoa	110	3¾
1 cup cornflour	125	4½
1 cup cornflakes, rice bubbles	30	1
1 cup coconut, desiccated	95	3¼
1 cup dried split peas, lentils	200	7
1 cup dried fruit	160	5¾
1 cup dates, chopped	150	5¼
1 cup flour, plain, SR	125	4½
1 cup flour, wholemeal	135	4¾
1 cup golden syrup, honey, glucose	360	12¾
1 cup jam	330	11½
1 cup nuts, chopped	125	4½
1 cup oats, rolled	90	3¼
1 cup rice, raw short grain	210	7½
1 cup rice, raw long grain	200	7
1 cup salt, or crystal sugar	250	8¾
1 cup castor sugar	220	7¾
1 cup soft brown sugar, firmly packed	170	6
1 cup icing sugar	150	5

OVEN TEMPERATURES	CELCIUS	FAHRENHEIT
Very hot	230-250	450-500
Hot	200-210	400-425
Moderate to moderately hot	180-190	350-375
Slow to moderately slow	150-160	300-325
Very slow	120	250

If using a fan-forced oven the temperature may vary somewhere between 15-20°C less than the above temperatures. Cooking time is also less in a fan-forced oven. For the correct temperatures please check with your oven handbook.

METRIC SPOONS	GRAMS	OUNCES
1 level tablespoon butter, peanut butter	20	⅔
1 level tablespoon baking powder, bicarb soda, cream of tartar, gelatine, rice, sago	15	½
1 level tablespoon cocoa, cornflour, custard powder, nuts	10	⅓
1 level tablespoon golden syrup, treacle, honey, glucose	30	1
1 level tablespoon sugar, salt	20	⅔
1 level tablespoon yeast, compressed	20	⅔
1 level tablespoon yeast, dry	10	⅓

AUSTRALIAN STANDARD METRIC CUPS AND SPOONS USED TO TEST

1 cup = 250 mls

1 tablespoon = 20 mls

1 teaspoon = 5 mls

THE FIRST COURSE

Velvety smooth cream soups of butternut pumpkin, carrot and sweet corn are some of the delicious vegetable soups in this chapter, always good choices for winter.

Interesting salads as a first course during summer are featuring more often these days on Australian menus, especially now with all the new varieties of lettuce.

The passion for pasta that has swept the country makes it a natural choice for an interesting first course. As well, there are some interesting little entrées and pre-dinner appetisers.

Red salmon mousse, page 12.

11

RED SALMON MOUSSE

Serve this as a first course or for parties to spread onto crispy biscuits.

2 220 g (7 oz) cans red salmon
2 sachets (or 1½ level tablespoons) gelatine
½ cup hot water
300 g (10 oz) carton sour cream
½ cup mayonnaise
½ cup tomato juice
pinch of cayenne
1 level tablespoon white onion, finely grated
½ cup celery, very finely diced

Put salmon and liquid from cans into a mixing bowl. Remove dark skin and any bones. Beat salmon with a fork. Dissolve gelatine in water and stir into the salmon with sour cream, mayonnaise, tomato juice, cayenne and onion. Beat well together then fold through the celery. Taste, adjust the flavours, then pack into a suitable mould and refrigerate until firmly set.
To unmould, dip mould briefly into warm water then turn out onto a flat platter. Cut into thick slices.
For an attractive garnish use dill, a few baby lettuce leaves and tiny tomatoes and serve with green goddess dressing or pureed avocado (seasoned with salt and spiked with chilli). Serves 8-10.

SALMON PATE

Arrange the mousse on a flat platter and serve as you would a pâté with crisp biscuits or rice crackers plus a small knife for spreading.

CREAM OF CARROT SOUP

This soup has a wonderful colour and makes a pleasant change from the usual pumpkin soup.

1 large onion, peeled and sliced
30 g (1 oz) butter
750 g (1½ lb) carrots, peeled and chopped
375 g (¾ lb) pumpkin, peeled and chopped
250 g (½ lb) ripe tomatoes
2 litres (8 cups) water
1 level teaspoon salt (or to taste)
pinch of dried tarragon
thickened cream
chives or mint, chopped

Place the prepared onion and butter into a large saucepan. Fry gently until onions are soft and glossy and tinged golden (slow and thorough cooking of the onions develops flavour). Add the carrot, pumpkin, chopped tomato, water, salt and tarragon. Cover the pan and simmer until vegetables are very soft, about ½ hour. Strain, reserving the liquid. Smooth out vegetables in a food processor, adding some of the liquid to keep blades spinning (if using a blender, cool down first). Return the purée and all liquid to the saucepan. Reheat, taste and adjust seasonings and consistency. Serve, adding a teaspoonful of softly whipped cream in each bowl. Sprinkle with chopped chives or mint. Serves 8.

TASMANIAN SCALLOP SOUP

This smooth cream-style soup has a most delicious flavour.

375 g (¾ lb) Tasmanian scallops
3 cups fish stock, court-bouillon or water
60 g (2 oz) butter
2 tablespoons shallot bulbs, chopped
½ level teaspoon curry powder
3 level tablespoons plain flour
2-3 level teaspoons tomato paste
¾ cup cream
chives to garnish

Poach the scallops for 2-3 minutes only in the fish stock or court-bouillon. If using water, add 1 small chicken cube for extra flavour.

Strain the scallops and save the liquid. Melt the butter in a saucepan, add the shallots and fry very gently for 3-4 minutes. Stir in the curry powder, cook a minute longer, then add the flour to make a roux. Cook over low heat for a few seconds, then add the scallop cooking liquid and tomato paste. Stir until the mixture boils and thickens, lower the heat, then stir in the cream and sliced or chopped scallops. Allow to heat through. Taste, adding a little salt if necessary. Serve sprinkled with chopped chives. Serves 6.

COURT-BOUILLON

A flavoured liquid used for poaching fish.

1 white onion, peeled and
chopped
1 carrot, peeled and
chopped
2 sticks celery, chopped
¼ teaspoon dried thyme
¼ teaspoon dried tarragon
¼ teaspoon fennel seeds
¼ bayleaf
½ level teaspoon salt
a few black peppercorns
½ cup dry white wine
6 cups water

Put all ingredients into a large saucepan and simmer for 30 minutes. Strain.

FRENCH ONION SOUP

A soup that has featured on many a 'blackboard menu'. I've always loved it, but it needs a really rich beef stock and the onions must be cooked very slowly in the butter first to develop a good flavour.

6 medium sized onions, peeled and sliced
1 heaped tablespoon butter (or ½ butter and ½ oil)
2 level tablespoons plain flour
6 cups rich beef stock
6 slices French bread, cut 1 cm (½ inch) thick
freshly ground black pepper
cheese, grated

Put onions and butter into a heavy based saucepan and fry gently for about ½ hour, stirring from time to time. The onions should be soft, glossy and a rich golden brown. Keep the heat low so they don't burn. Sprinkle in the flour, stir well, then add the stock. Stir until boiling, then lower the heat and simmer gently for about 20 minutes. Meanwhile, put the bread slices onto a baking tray and bake in a moderate oven for 20 minutes or until crisp. Season soup to taste with salt and lots of black pepper. Pour into a casserole dish or 6 individual ramekins. Top with the crisp bread, sprinkle over the cheese, and bake for a further 10 minutes in a moderate oven. Serves 6.

RICH BEEF STOCK

Good cooks are starting to come back to the old ways of making a 'proper' stock as a basis for soups and sauces when it is for something special.
Use meats and some of the stock to make an old fashioned brawn.

500 g (1 lb) shin of beef
2 veal knuckles
1 medium carrot
1 onion, peeled
1 stick celery
1 clove garlic, peeled
¾ cup dry white wine
2½ litres (10 cups) water
1 large ripe tomato
1 teaspoon tomato paste
1 bouquet garni (bayleaf, parsley, thyme tied to a piece of celery)
a few peppercorns

Put chunks of beef and veal knuckles into a lightly buttered baking dish. Put into a hot oven and brown well. Add roughly chopped carrot, onion, celery and whole clove garlic. Cook without browning for about 10 minutes, then empty into a very large saucepan or boiler. Swill out baking dish with wine to include meat drippings. Add to the pot and boil rapidly over a high heat until it is mostly evaporated. Add water, whole tomato, tomato paste, bouquet garni and peppercorns. Cook slowly for about 3-4 hours. Skim from time to time as necessary. Strain and refrigerate.

OLD-FASHIONED BRAWN

Remove meats from the rich beef stock and shred *very finely* using two forks. Arrange a sliced hardboiled egg in the bottom of a small basin. Pack the shredded meat into the basin with chopped parsley, fresh milled pepper and a light sprinkling of salt. Heat 1 cup of the stock and boil to reduce slightly, season with a dash Worcestershire sauce, and a little dry mustard, cayenne pepper and grated nutmeg. Add a good squeeze of lemon juice and pour into the basin to barely cover the meat. Cover with a saucer. Weight down and refrigerate until set.

SWEET CORN SOUP

1 white onion, peeled and
finely chopped
2 level tablespoons butter
1 can (440 g) sweet corn
kernels
2 level tablespoons plain
flour
2¼ cups milk
¼ cup cream
½ level teaspoon salt
freshly ground pepper
2 bacon rashers, chopped
parsley or chives, chopped

Put onion and butter into a saucepan and fry gently for 10 minutes or until the onion is soft and just starting to turn golden (slow cooking of onions in butter at this stage develops a good flavour). Meanwhile, drain corn kernels and chop roughly (use food processor). Add to the onion with the flour and stir well before adding the milk and cream. Stir constantly until the mixture boils and thickens. Add the salt and pepper to taste. A little extra milk or cream may be added to thin if necessary. Serve soup sprinkled with chopped grilled bacon and chopped parsley or chives. Serves 4.

CREAM OF MUSHROOM SOUP

250 g (½ lb) large flat
mushrooms (although
cultivated they are
sometimes called field
mushrooms)
¼ cup shallots (white bulbs
only) sliced or 1 tiny white
onion, finely chopped
2 heaped tablespoons butter
¼ level teaspoon curry
powder
2 level tablespoons plain
flour
3 cups milk
salt and freshly ground
pepper
¼ cup cream
green shallot tops or chives,
finely sliced

Trim away any tough parts of the mushroom stems. Slice mushrooms. Put shallots and butter into a large saucepan, sauté for a few minutes until soft, then add the mushrooms and curry powder. Fry fairly quickly on both sides, then sprinkle in the flour. Mix through the mushrooms, then stir in the milk. Stir until the mixture boils, then reduce the heat and simmer for a good 15-20 minutes. Smooth out in a food processor (if using a blender, cool first). Return soup to the pan to reheat, then add cream and season to taste with salt and pepper. Serve topped with chopped chives or young shallot tops. Serves 5.

BUTTERNUT PUMPKIN SOUP

30 g (1 oz) butter
1 onion, peeled and sliced
1 kg (2 lb) butternut
pumpkin
1½ litres (6 cups) chicken
stock or water
½ level teaspoon salt
pinch of nutmeg
3-4 tablespoons cream
freshly ground black pepper
a little thickened cream
chives, chopped

Melt the butter in a saucepan. Add the onion and sauté over a low heat until it is soft and glossy – it takes about 10 minutes to develop a good flavour. Add the peeled and chopped pumpkin, chicken stock and salt. Bring to the boil, reduce the heat and cover the pan. Simmer for ¾ hour or until the pumpkin is very tender. Strain the mixture, reserving the liquid. Smooth out pumpkin in a food processor, adding sufficient liquid to keep the machine spinning (if using a blender, cool first). Return the purée and liquid to the pan and reheat. Add freshly ground pepper, nutmeg and cream. Taste, and adjust seasonings and consistency. Ladle into soup bowls (or use a hollowed out bush pumpkin shell). Add a little swirl of cream and a sprinkle of chives. Serves 8.
Note: The bush pumpkin shell used for serving is not cooked.

Opposite: Butternut pumpkin soup.

GOLD COAST PRAWN SALAD

This is a good choice when entertaining friends from overseas. Serve on a large platter or on individual plates.

1 kg (2 lb) medium king prawns, peeled with tails attached
lemon dressing (page 24)
1 red banana capsicum (or ½ red capsicum)
1 medium sized carrot
2 sticks celery (choose tender sticks from near the centre)
1 tub alfalfa
baby lettuce leaves, washed and crisped
2 firm ripe avocados
1 large mango or ½ pawpaw, peeled and cut into thick slices
parsley, chopped

Place the peeled prawns into a bowl and pour over the lemon dressing. Cover and refrigerate for 1 hour (2 hours at the most).

Cut the capsicum, carrot and celery into fine shreds, then place into a bowl of iced water. Before serving, drain the vegetables and the prawns, (but reserve dressing). Peel and slice the avocado and arrange with the fruit, crispy vegetables and lettuce on a large platter or individual plates. Add the prawns and little bouquets of alfalfa. Drizzle over the lemon dressing and sprinkle with parsley. Serves 6. I often serve this informally on a large platter (especially if catering for more than 6) accompanied by dainty finger sandwiches of wholegrain bread.

Opposite: Gold Coast prawn salad.

LEMON DRESSING

1 lemon
1 tiny clove garlic
½ teaspoon mixed French or German mustard
3 tablespoons oil
salt and freshly ground black pepper

Remove a couple of paper thin strips of lemon peel with a potato peeler or sharp knife. Cut into fine strips. Crush the garlic and put into a bowl, stir in the mustard, then add 1 tablespoon lemon juice and the oil. Add a pinch of salt and freshly ground black pepper, mix well, and add the lemon peel.

HOT AVOCADO SEAFOOD

You'll need a set of ovenproof avocado dishes for this recipe. It's almost a meal, so plan a very light main course to follow.

2 small to medium avocados (firmly ripe)
250 g (½ lb) Tasmanian scallops
½ cup dry white wine
½ cup water
60 g (2 oz) butter
6 shallots, trimmed and chopped
2 cups (about 125 g or ¼ lb) button mushrooms, sliced
2 level tablespoons plain flour
1 cup milk
⅓ cup reserved scallop liquid
pepper and salt
dash of tabasco

2 tablespoons parsley,
chopped
½ cup tasty cheese, grated
1 bacon rasher, trimmed
then finely chopped

Trim black beards from scallops and poach in wine and water for 3 minutes only. Remove scallops with a slotted spoon and reserve. Boil scallop broth rapidly until reduced to ⅓ cup. Heat butter in a separate saucepan, add shallots and mushrooms and fry gently until mushrooms soften. Add flour and mix well. Add milk and ⅓ cup scallop liquid. Stir until sauce boils and thickens. Add poached scallops and parsley. Season to taste with pepper, salt and tabasco. Heat oven to hot. Cut avocados into halves, remove skins carefully, then remove seeds. Put avocado halves into individual avocado dishes and spoon over the creamed scallop mixture. Sprinkle with grated cheese and scatter over the bacon. Place in a baking dish and bake in the preheated oven for 8-10 minutes – no longer. The avocados should simply be warmed; if overheated they lose their smooth texture and sweet flavour. Serves 4 for an entrée or light lunch.

SALMON SALAD

Niçoise-style salad makes a pretty first course arranged in a shallow bowl. It is especially good served outdoors for a summery lunch.

500 g (1 lb) potatoes
1 fat clove garlic
1 level teaspoon smooth French or German mustard
2 tablespoons lemon juice
3 or 4 tablespoons oil
250 g (½ lb) stringless green beans, topped, tailed and boiled until crisp
1 Granny Smith apple, peeled and chopped
1 mignonette lettuce
1 can good red salmon
1 tiny white mild-flavoured onion, sliced paper thin
4 hard-boiled eggs
2 small tomatoes
1 tablespoon parsley, chopped
1 tablespoon chives, chopped
1 teaspoon mint or basil, chopped

Peel potatoes and cut into thickish slices. Boil until crispy tender (about 8 to 10 minutes). Drain and leave to cool. Crush garlic and place into a bowl. Add mustard and lemon juice. Gradually stir in oil to make a dressing. Add cold potatoes, beans and apple. Toss lightly and place in the bottom of a lettuce-lined bowl. Put drained salmon in centre and scatter over onion. Arrange wedges of egg and tomato around the outside. Pour over any dressing remaining in the bowl and sprinkle salad with chopped herbs. Serves 4-5.

DIM SIMS

*For a more authentic
Chinese flavour use
Chinese dried mushrooms
soaked in warm water
then squeezed dry. To
make the Chinese
mushrooms taste
especially good, after
squeezing dry place them
into a small saucepan
with 1 tablespoon water,
1 teaspoon soy sauce and
a pinch of sugar. Simmer,
stirring occasionally,
until all liquid
evaporates. Cool before
mincing or chopping.*

**1 packet short soup covers
(little squares of noodle
paste, also known as won
tun skins, available from
Chinese grocers)
250 g (½ lb) pork fillet
250 g (½ lb) raw prawns,
peeled
6-8 firm button mushrooms
8 canned water chestnuts
6 shallots, excluding green
leaves
2 level teaspoons salt (or to
taste)
1 level teaspoon sugar
1 tablespoon soy sauce**

Mince pork, prawns, mushrooms, water chestnuts and
shallots in food processor. Empty into a bowl, add salt,
sugar and soy sauce. Beat with chopsticks or a fork until
thoroughly mixed. Put a teaspoon of the mixture on the
centre of each pastry square and squeeze near the top of
pastry so that it resembles a little money bag, then pat
down on bench to flatten base. Oil base of Chinese bamboo
steaming baskets (there are usually enough dim sims for
two baskets). Arrange dim sims into basket with room
between so they don't touch. Cover with lid and place
steamer over a wok of simmering water for about 15
minutes. Serve hot with a dipping sauce of light soy and
toasted sesame seeds. Serve hot as a first course.
Wrap any leftover pastry in plastic and store in freezer.

SINGAPORE SATAY WITH PEANUT SAUCE

*1 kg (2 lb) lean pork (pork
neck, sometimes called
'scotch fillet' is a wonderful
juicy cut to use for satay)
1 small white onion, finely
chopped
1 clove garlic, crushed
2 teaspoons coriander
2 teaspoons cummin
1 teaspoon fresh ginger,
grated
small piece lemon grass,
white butt only, thinly
sliced (or substitute ½
teaspoon lemon rind,
grated)
2 tablespoons oil
1 tablespoon soy sauce
2 teaspoons brown sugar*

Cut meat into small cubes. Place into a bowl with
remaining ingredients and mix thoroughly. Cover and place
in refrigerator to marinate for an hour or so or overnight.
Thread onto bamboo skewers and fry gently in a little
butter in a frypan or on a barbecue plate. Serve with
peanut sauce, sliced cucumber and lettuce. Serves 5-6.

PEANUT SAUCE

1 small onion, finely sliced
2 cloves garlic, crushed
2 tablespoons oil
2 tablespoons lemon juice
1 tablespoon brown sugar
(or to taste)
2 heaped tablespoons
crunchy peanut butter
1 teaspoon soy sauce
1 cup water
dash of chilli sauce
good pinch of Chinese five
spice
½ cup coconut milk
(optional)
salt to taste

Sauté onion and garlic in oil until well cooked, then add lemon juice, sugar, peanut butter, soy and water. Simmer for about 5 minutes or more, then add chilli sauce and five spice. Thin with coconut milk and simmer a little longer. Add salt to taste. Adjust seasonings and serve in a bowl with satay.

ASPARAGUS AND BACON GRATIN

6 small eggs
2 tablespoons butter
3 level tablespoons plain
flour
2 cups milk
2-3 tablespoons cream
1 heaped teaspoon smooth
Dijon-style mustard
1 can (440 g) green
asparagus spears, drained
250 g (½ lb) bacon rashers,
chopped, cooked and
drained
1½ cups soft white or
wholegrain breadcrumbs,
tossed in a little melted
butter or bacon fat

Boil eggs for 10 minutes, drain and remove shells under cold running water. Melt butter in a saucepan, add flour to form a roux, then add milk and cream. Stir until sauce boils and thickens. Add mustard, salt and pepper. Cut eggs into halves or quarters and add to the sauce with asparagus (chopped in halves) and cooked bacon. Put into a shallow gratin dish or individual dishes. Sprinkle over buttered crumbs and bake in a hot oven for about 10 minutes or until crumbs are golden. Serves 6 as an entrée.

BACON AND MUSHROOM FETTUCCINE

Luscious fettuccine noodles in a creamy sauce with mushrooms and bacon

250 g (½ lb) dried fettuccine noodles (allow 375 g (¾ lb) or more if using fresh pasta)
75 g (2½ oz) butter
½ cup shallots, chopped
3 or 4 bacon rashers, chopped (excess fat trimmed away)
125 g (4 oz) firm button mushrooms, sliced
4 tablespoons fresh cream
2 tablespoons water
½ cup mature cheddar cheese, grated
freshly ground black pepper
fresh basil or parsley, chopped

Cook pasta in boiling salted water until cooked (time depends on type used). Melt butter in a frying pan, fry shallots for a few minutes, then add bacon. Fry for a few minutes more, then push to one side of the pan and add the mushrooms. Fry quickly until mushrooms soften, then add cream and water. Simmer for a minute or so to create a sauce. Add drained pasta and cheese and toss together. Add an extra tablespoon cream and water if necessary to lighten. Serve sprinkled with black pepper and chopped basil. Serves 4.

FISH

Freshly caught fish with the smell of the sea, cooked lightly and dressed simply with butter and lemon, is a memorable taste. A trip to the fish markets is the next best thing to catching it yourself and due to the influence of Asian, Middle Eastern and Continental communities in Australia, the choice of fish available these days is dazzling.

A selection of Australian seafood: garfish, sea bream, silver bream, snapper, octopus, oysters, mussels and pipis.

AUSTRALIAN BOUILLABAISSE

The Mediterranean bouillabaisse adapts readily to the fish and seafood available in Australia. The result is a distinctly Australian bouillabaisse.

**3 leeks, well washed
3 tablespoons oil
2 large cloves garlic
4 large ripe tomatoes, chopped
3 level tablespoons tomato paste
2 litres (8 cups) fish stock (the recipe is on page 53)
pinch of salt
freshly ground black pepper
thin strip of orange peel
2 good pinches of fennel seeds
1 level teaspoon dried basil leaves
1 kg (2 lb) filleted fish
1 kg (2 lb) green prawns (include washed heads and shells in stock)
500 g (1 lb) well scrubbed mussels
250 g (½ lb) Tasmanian scallops
½ cup Italian parsley and/or fresh basil, chopped
1 or 2 crispy French loaves
1 recipe for rouille (see following)**

Remove the green leaves before slicing the leeks. Place them with the oil and garlic into a large boiler.
Sauté gently for 5-10 minutes, then add tomatoes and tomato paste. Pour in strained fish stock, then add a good pinch of salt and grind in lots of black pepper. Add the orange peel after removing any white pith, fennel seeds and

basil. Increase the heat and bring to the boil, watching carefully to prevent it boiling over. Continue boiling for 5-10 minutes to amalgamate the broth. Lower the heat and add fish, peeled prawns and mussels. Cover and simmer gently until the mussels open. This will take 5-6 minutes, then add the scallops and cook a few minutes longer. Taste, add more salt if necessary.

Serve in big shallow soup bowls or spaghetti dishes sprinkled with parsley and fresh basil when it is in season. Serve with hot crusty French bread slices and a bowl of Rouille. Serves 8-10.

ROUILLE

Once addicted to this, it is hard to leave it alone!

5 slices white bread, crusts removed
4 tablespoons fish stock
2 fresh red chillies
4 large cloves garlic
1 level tablespoon tomato paste
2 egg yolks
¾ cup salad oil or olive if you prefer
extra ¼ cup fish stock

Soak bread in the fish stock.

Halve chillies, remove seeds under cold running water (wash hands well after handling chillies). Put chillies into food processor or blender goblet with peeled garlic and mince finely. Add soaked bread and process until smooth. Add tomato paste and egg yolks. While the machine is running add the oil, drop by drop at first just as if making mayonnaise, then increase to a thin steady stream. When all has been added the mixture should be thick and creamy. Add the fish stock very gradually as this will lighten the rouille. Transfer to a bowl and cover tightly with plastic. Covering is necessary as the top surface will discolour if left open to air. Refrigerate until ready to serve.

SNOWY MOUNTAIN TROUT WITH ALMONDS

2 packets frozen rainbow
trout (each 375 g (12 oz)
packet contains 2 plate-
sized trout)
salt and pepper to taste
a little plain flour
100 g (3½ oz) butter
¼ cup of blanched and split
almonds,
juice of 1 lemon
1 heaped tablespoon fresh
parsley, chopped

Thaw trout in refrigerator. Remove head and skin (grasp head and simply pull down towards the tail – the skin peels away beautifully in one operation). Season trout with salt and pepper and dust lightly with flour.
Fry gently in butter, turning once. Remove to heated plates. Add almonds to butter (add extra if necessary) and toss quickly until golden. Add lemon juice and chopped parsley. Pour over trout and serve immediately. Serves 4.

SMOKED FISH PATTIES

500 g (1 lb) smoked cod or
haddock, skinned
500 g (1 lb) potatoes
1 cup grated tasty cheese
rind and juice of 1 large
lemon
1 tablespoon finely grated
white onion
1 level teaspoon horseradish
relish
1 egg
flour, egg and dry
breadcrumbs

Put skinned fish into a frying pan and cover with water, bring to the boil, then pour away the water and replace with fresh cold water. Return to heat and simmer gently for about 10 minutes, then cool, drain and flake. Meanwhile, peel potatoes and cook in boiling water until tender, drain and mash well, then add flaked fish, cheese, lemon rind and juice, onion, horseradish and egg. Mix well, then form into small patties or into balls. Roll in plain flour then beaten egg and dry crumbs. Deep fry until thoroughly hot and the outside is crisp and golden. Serve with horseradish sauce (the recipe is on page 73). Serves 4-5.

FISH FILLETS CAPRICORN

1 kg (2 lb) fish fillets (snapper
or perch are especially good)
salt and pepper
2 level tablespoons plain flour
2 eggs
1-1¼ cups desiccated coconut or
a mixture of ½ dry
breadcrumbs and ½ coconut
60 g (2 oz) butter
juice of 1 lemon
natural yoghurt
chives

Season the fish with salt and pepper and then dip into
plain flour. Shake off excess flour, then dip into beaten egg
and then into coconut. Pat crust on firmly. Heat butter in a
shallow frying pan and, keeping the heat very low, fry the
fish (the coconut catches very quickly so the heat must be
very gentle). Towards the end of the cooking squeeze over
the lemon juice. Serve topped with a little natural yoghurt
and sprinkled with chives. Delicious with a green salad or
cucumber salad and boiled rice or tiny new potatoes.
Serves 6.

SALMON FRITTERS (MOCK FISH)

A leftover from the austerity years during the Second World War. I love the way the potatoes become crisp and brown on the outside while the inside is moist and creamy.

1 medium can (around 200 g) pink salmon or tuna
2 eggs
4 level tablespoons SR flour
1 heaped tablespoon parsley, chopped
1 white onion, peeled and grated coarsely
1 small carrot, peeled and grated coarsely
2 cups potato (prepare just before cooking), coarsely grated
½ level teaspoon salt
freshly ground black pepper
2 lemons

Empty the can of fish including the liquid into a bowl, add unbeaten eggs, flour, parsley, onion, carrot and potato. (Grated potato discolours quickly so it should be added to the mixture just before cooking). Add salt and lots of freshly ground black pepper. Heat sufficient oil in a large pan to shallow fry the fritters. Drop mixture into hot oil in level tablespoons. When golden on both sides, drain very well on absorbent paper towels and squeeze over the juice of 1 lemon. Serve immediately with extra lemon wedges. Makes about 18-20. Serves about 5.

LOBSTER THERMIDOR

*1 medium sized cooked
lobster
½ cup shallots (white butts
only), chopped
3 level tablespoons butter
125 g (4 oz) baby button
mushrooms
2 level tablespoons flour
¾ cup milk
2-3 tablespoons cream
¼ cup dry white wine
1 level teaspoon smooth
French mixed mustard
salt and pepper
1 cup soft breadcrumbs,
tossed in a little melted butter
1 tablespoon grated parmesan
or romano cheese (optional)*

HOW TO PREPARE A COOKED LOBSTER

Place a sharp knife halfway down the underside of the lobster and cut, levering the knife towards the tail. Turn the lobster around and cut towards the head. Open into halves and remove the flesh, discard the vein. Rinse shells. Sauté shallots gently in butter then add finely sliced mushrooms. Cook over a low heat for a few minutes, then sprinkle with flour. Mix well and then stir in milk and cream. Continue to stir until the sauce boils and thickens, then add the wine and lower the heat. Slice the lobster flesh and add to the sauce. Heat through, then add the mustard and season with a small pinch of salt and freshly ground pepper. Spoon into clean lobster shells and sprinkle with buttered crumbs and cheese. Place under the griller to lightly brown and crisp topping. Serves 2.

CURRIED PRAWNS

1 kg (2 lb) green prawns, shelled
30 g (1 oz) butter
1 large onion, halved then finely sliced
2 large cloves garlic, crushed
½ red capsicum, sliced (optional)
1 level tablespoon curry powder
1 level teaspoon ground coriander
2 large ripe tomatoes, peeled
1 cup water
1 teaspoon green ginger, grated
stick of cinnamon
pepper and salt
juice of ½ lemon
60 g (2 oz) creamed coconut

Wash and de-vein prawns. Melt the butter in a frying pan and add onion, garlic and capsicum. Fry gently for 10 minutes, keeping the vegetables transparent, then add curry powder and coriander and fry gently a few minutes longer. Now add chopped tomatoes, water, ginger, cinnamon stick and a good pinch of salt. Simmer gently for 15 minutes, then add peeled prawns, a little ground pepper and lemon juice. Simmer until prawns are cooked, approximately 3-4 minutes. Chop coconut cream and stir into the sauce until dissolved. Serve with boiled rice and a side dish of sliced cucumber in yoghurt, sprinkled with chopped chives or baby shallot tops. Serves 4.

HONEY PRAWNS

This is a popular dish in Chinese restaurants and easy to make at home.

1½ kg (3 lb) raw king prawns, with tail section still attached, peeled
crunchy batter (the recipe is on page 52)
3-4 level tablespoons honey
3 chillies, seeds removed and sliced into fine slivers
toasted sesame seeds

De-vein the prawns, rinse under cold running water, then pat dry. Dust very lightly with a little flour then dip into the batter. Test one prawn first and if the batter seems a little too thick thin down by adding extra water. Deep fry prawns in the batter for a few minutes until cooked. Drain on paper towels. Heat the honey gently in a wok or frying pan until it is melted and add the chillies and cooked prawns. Toss quickly over a moderate heat to coat prawns then sprinkle with sesame seeds and serve immediately. Serves 6.

Note: To toast sesame seeds put into a dry pan and heat until they turn golden shaking or stirring constantly. They burn easily so keep an eye on them. Toasted black sesame seeds are sometimes used for honey prawns.

Opposite: fish, scallops and prawns in a crunchy batter, page 52.

SEAFOOD ST HELENS

Serve this delicious dish sprinkled with parsley or chives and garnished with a small sprig of fennel.

1 kg (2 lb) medium sized cooked king prawns
500 g (1 lb) Tasmanian scallops
½ cup white wine
1 cup water
a few peppercorns
½ teaspoon fennel seeds
90 g (3 oz) butter
½ cup shallots (discarding green stems), chopped
250 g (½ lb) button mushrooms, sliced
4 level tablespoons plain flour
2-2½ cups milk
1 level teaspoon tomato paste
salt, pepper and cayenne
1-2 tablespoons cream
parsley or chives, chopped
sprig of fresh fennel to garnish

Peel and de-vein prawns. Cover and refrigerate until needed. Remove and discard the black thread-like beard from the scallops, then poach them in wine and water with the peppercorns and fennel seeds for 3 minutes only. Remove scallops with a slotted spoon to a bowl. Boil scallop liquid rapidly and reduce by half to concentrate flavour. Melt butter, add shallots and mushrooms, fry for few minutes then stir in flour.

Add 2 cups milk and ¾ cup reduced scallop liquid. Bring to boil, stirring constantly, then beat. The sauce should be very smooth and shiny. Stir in the tomato paste, then add

Opposite: Seafood St Helens

the prawns and scallops. Heat gently. Add salt, pepper and a good pinch of cayenne. Taste, adjust seasonings, and thin if necessary with extra milk or cream. Serves 6-8.

WITH A CRISPY TOPPING

Combine soft white breadcrumbs with chopped parsley, a little soft butter and a few drops of garlic juice. Put prawn and scallop mixture into a shallow dish. Sprinkle with crumbs and bake in a very hot oven until the sauce bubbles and the top is crispy and golden brown.

ALMOND CRUSTED FILLETS WITH SPECIAL SAUCE

Juicy flathead fillets encrusted with crisp golden almonds and served with a delicious sweet and sour sauce.

6 large flathead fillets
2.5 cm (1 inch) piece of green ginger
1 small clove garlic, crushed
1 egg, beaten
¾ cup SR flour
¾ cup water
185-250 g (6-8 oz) slivered or flaked almonds
oil to deep fry
lemon or lime quarters for serving

Remove skin from fish.* Trim away the little section of bones usually attached to flathead fillets, then halve each fillet lengthways and place into a dish. Peel and grate ginger then squeeze to extract the juice. Add this ginger juice to the fish with a little crushed garlic and the egg and marinate for ½ hour. Meanwhile, chop almonds finely with a sharp knife or food processor and spread half the almonds onto a plate (you will see the wisdom of this later). Make a batter with SR flour and water. Add to the fillets and mix around to coat well. Remove pieces of fish one at a time and dip into almonds, coating both sides, then deep fry in oil. When more almonds are needed to coat fish, spread out onto a fresh dry plate. Drain cooked fish on paper towels and serve hot with lime or lemon quarters, plain boiled rice and special sauce. This dish looks wonderful when presented on a bright green banana leaf. Serves 4-6.

*To skin fish: Work with skin side to the board and narrow end towards you. Slip knife between skin and fish, then grip the skin in one hand and slide the knife along, pulling the skin with a zig-zag movement. Use a little salt on your fingers if the skin is slippery.

SPECIAL SAUCE

2 level tablespoons tomato sauce
1 teaspoon Worcestershire sauce
1 cup pineapple juice
1 heaped teaspoon sugar
2 level teaspoons cornflour
a few drops of ginger juice (grate ginger and press through garlic crusher)

Combine all ingredients in a saucepan, stir to mix in cornflour thoroughly, then bring to the boil, stirring constantly. Simmer for few minutes. Pour into bowl. It is delicious hot or cold.

BARBECUED MULLET

As it is an oily fish, mullet is particularly good when cooked over a barbecue fire.

Clean, scale, remove head, and cut right down to the tail so that the whole fish opens out flat. Alternatively, use mullet fillets. Place between a hinged 'boy scout' griller (greasing griller first to stop sticking). Brush lightly with oil or butter and barbecue slowly over ashes (not a fierce fire). When cooked, score the flesh with a small sharp knife and squeeze over lemon juice. Leave on the barbecue for a minute or so, then season with salt and freshly ground pepper and serve with lemon wedges.

GARFISH

These sweet and tender little fish have a delicate flavour and snowy white flesh. They're well worth the extra trouble in preparation.

Garfish are sold whole and ungutted and are usually inexpensive to buy. To prepare garfish, slit open from head to tail and scrape out the contents of the cavity. Use a dessertspoon, gently scrape away the black skin inside the stomach, then rinse fish and pat dry. Remove head and open the little fish out flat. Roll with a milk bottle or press down gently with heel of hand, then remove the backbone. For fussy eaters, it is just as well to slip a knife under any tiny bones at the edges and remove also. Just before serving, dip into flour, then fry gently in a little butter for one or two minutes only. Add a big squeeze of fresh lemon or lime juice to the pan and serve immediately.

SAUCES FOR SEAFOOD

CLASSIC MAYONNAISE

This mayonnaise is thick and luscious and perfect to serve with shellfish or thick chunks of juicy ham or simply to mask a perfectly fresh hard-boiled egg.

2 egg yolks
½ level teaspoon salt (or to taste)
¼ level teaspoon dry mustard or 1 level teaspoon smooth French mustard
2 tablespoons white vinegar (or use strained fresh lemon juice)
1¼ cups oil (measured into a good pouring jug)
tiny pinch of white pepper

Put yolks, salt and mustard into a bowl. Beat for a few minutes with a small balloon whisk until thick and sticky. Add 1 tablespoon vinegar and beat in well. Add oil, *drop by drop* at first, whisking constantly. After half the oil has been added the mixture should be starting to thicken and the critical time is over. Whisk in remaining oil (pour in a thin steady stream). Adjust flavours, adding the extra vinegar and more salt if necessary and the white pepper.

Note: This mayonnaise could be beaten in the small bowl of an electric mixer providing the same rule applies when adding the oil, drop by drop at first.

Curdled Mayonnaise happens if the oil is added too quickly. Here's how to save it: Put a fresh egg yolk into a clean bowl then gradually add the curdled mixture (drop by drop at first) until all has been added.

CLASSIC MAYONNAISE IN FOOD PROCESSOR

This recipe works beautifully and is so quick and easy to make.

2 eggs
½ level teaspoon salt
1 teaspoon smooth prepared mustard
2 tablespoons white vinegar
2 cups salad oil
pinch of cayenne pepper

Place eggs, salt and mustard into food processor bowl. Add ½ tablespoon vinegar and process for a few seconds. Pour oil into a measuring jug. Start machine and begin to add the oil, drop by drop at first, then in a thin steady stream until 1 cup has been added. Turn machine off and rest for a second then beat in 1 tablespoon more vinegar and gradually add remaining oil. Add remaining ½ tablespoon vinegar plus cayenne. Taste, adjust flavours, adding a touch more vinegar if necessary. Pour into a container and cover tightly. Refrigerate until needed.

Note: Although this is a very easy mayonnaise to make, the food processor isn't magic and it is still necessary to add oil very gradually at first.

TARTARE SAUCE

1 cup mayonnaise
3 shallots, chopped (exclude green stems)
1 tablespoon capers
1 tablespoon gherkin, finely chopped
few drops of garlic juice (optional)
1 tablespoon parsley, chopped
good squeeze of lemon juice

Combine all ingredients. Cover and refrigerate for an hour or so to allow the flavours to mingle.

GREEN GODDESS DRESSING FOR SHELLFISH

This is a lovely sauce for dunking prawns or lobster.

4 anchovy fillets, finely chopped
6 young shallots, finely chopped and including the green stems
½ level teaspoon dried tarragon
¼ cup each Italian parsley and chives, chopped
clove garlic, crushed
1 cup classic mayonnaise (the recipe is on page 49)
dash of chilli sauce or a good pinch of cayenne

Place anchovies, shallots, herbs and garlic into a food processor and blend well. Add mayonnaise and chilli. Serve chilled.

BLENDER HOLLANDAISE

1 tablespoon lemon juice
4 egg yolks
¾-1 cup hot melted butter
salt and pepper

Put lemon juice and egg yolks into blender or food processor bowl and process for a couple of seconds to combine. With machine running, start to add the melted butter, drop by drop at first, then gradually increasing to a fine steady stream as you see the sauce starting to thicken. Season with salt and pepper to taste. This is especially good with hot steamed broccoli and asparagus and with poached fish.

BATTERS

BEER BATTER

This is very light and crispy and an excellent batter for seafood

¾ *cup plain flour*
good pinch of salt
1 small egg
2 teaspoons oil or melted butter
scant ¾ cup flat beer

Combine ingredients and beat thoroughly until smooth. Dip seafood into flour first, shaking off any excess. Now dip in the batter and place straight into the hot deep oil.

CRUNCHY BATTER

This batter seems to stay crisp longer than most and is specially good for fish or prawns

1 cup SR flour
¼ *cup cornflour*
good pinch of salt
1 cup water
good squeeze of lemon juice
1 tablespoon oil

Sift flour, cornflour and salt into a bowl. Add ¾ cup water, lemon juice and oil. Beat well until smooth, then gradually add the remaining water. If the batter is too thick, adjust the consistency by adding a few drops of extra water. Dust seafood very lightly with flour then dip into batter, drain any excess, then lower straight into deep hot oil.

EGG BATTER

Dip fish fillets into plain flour then straight into beaten egg and then into a shallow pan of hot oil. This batter forms a thin crinkly coating on fish. It is a nice batter when freshly cooked and also very good when cold and sprinkled with a little French dressing. A slice of green ginger and a flattened clove of garlic added to the oil when cooking fish this way also imparts a delicious subtle flavour.

FISH STOCK

1 kg (2 lb) fish bones and
trimmings
1 onion, peeled and roughly
chopped
½ cup dry white wine
2 litres (8 cups) water
mushroom peelings (optional)
1 stick celery, chopped
1 bay leaf
good pinch each of dried
thyme and fennel seeds
few sprigs parsley
good pinch of salt
1 lemon, cut into thick slices
few peppercorns and cloves

Place fish bones and trimmings into a large saucepan,
cover with water and soak to remove any blood. Drain off
this water. Put onion and wine into the pot and simmer
until the wine evaporates, shaking pot from time to time.
Add the water with the remaining ingredients and bring to
the boil. Simmer for 20 minutes only. Strain and refrigerate
or freeze until needed for cooking.

MAIN COURSES

*Perfect baked dinners and
homemade meat pies
with crumbly pastry that
melts in the mouth are
recipes that our mothers
and grandmothers
perfected.*
*Those recipes are in this
chapter as well as other
'traditional' favourites.
And, while we relate to
the food we loved as
children, there's a new
style of eating in
Australia today, a style
that reflects influences
from our multi-cultural
society as well as the new
way of fresh, light eating.*

*Roast lamb dinner,
page 70.*

MINESTRONE

500 g (1 lb) shin of beef
1 knuckle veal
1 tablespoon butter
2 onions, peeled and sliced
4 litres (16 cups) water
2 teaspoons salt
3 cloves garlic, crushed
1 carrot, peeled and diced
2 sticks celery, chopped
1 can peeled tomatoes
2 level tablespoons tomato
paste
1 can red kidney beans
1 cup fresh beans, chopped
1 cup spaghetti, broken into
pieces
¼ small cabbage, shredded
grated parmesan or cheddar
cheese

Brown meats in butter in a large boiler. Add onions, stir well and shake over heat until they soften. Add water and salt, then bring to the boil. Reduce heat and simmer for approximately 2 hours. Remove scum from the stock and sides of the pan with paper towels. Add garlic, carrot, celery, tinned tomatoes with the juice, tomato paste, kidney beans including the liquid in the can, fresh beans and spaghetti. Simmer for 20 minutes, adding cabbage during last 10 minutes of cooking. Remove the meat, chop roughly then return to soup with lots of freshly ground black pepper. Taste, adjust salt, reheat and serve sprinkled with cheese. Pass around warm crusty bread. Serves 10.

PEA SOUP

*As a variation, use 4 or 5
lamb knuckles in the
soup instead of the ham
bones.*

**500 g (1 lb) yellow split peas
2 onions, peeled and sliced
30 g (1 oz) butter
500 g (1 lb) carrots, peeled
and coarsely grated
¼ bunch celery, chopped
1 ham bone or a smoked
hock (or both)
4 litres (16 cups) water
½ teaspoon dried thyme or
few sprigs fresh thyme
salt and pepper to taste
fresh mint or parsley to
garnish, chopped**

Empty split peas into a boiler. Sauté onions in butter until
soft and glossy, then add to peas with carrots, celery and
ham bone or hock. Pour in water and add thyme. Place lid
on the boiler and simmer gently for approximately 2 hours,
stirring occasionally. Remove bones, chop meat and return
to the pot. Allow to heat through, taste and add freshly
ground pepper and, if necessary, a little salt. Serve hot
sprinkled with mint or parsley. Serves 10.

SCOTCH BROTH

*A good old vegetable
soup with lamb shanks
has a homely,
comfortable flavour.*

*2 large onions, peeled and
chopped*
30 g (1 oz) butter
6 lamb knuckles
4 litres (16 cups) water
*¾ cup dried soup mix
(mixture of split peas,
barley, lentils and alphabet
noodles)*
4 sticks celery, chopped
*3 large carrots, peeled and
diced*
1 parsnip, peeled and diced
*1 small turnip, peeled and
diced (optional)*
2 level teaspoons salt
freshly ground black pepper
lots of chopped parsley

Place onion and butter into a large saucepan or boiler. Fry
gently until soft then add the remaining ingredients (with
exception of the parsley) and simmer gently for 2 hours,
stirring occasionally. Serve topped with freshly ground
pepper and lots of chopped fresh parsley. Store leftovers in
refrigerator. Scotch broth may be made 24 hours before as
the flavour improves the next day. Serves 10.

SALT PORK

Tastes rather like a mild ham. Meat is a pretty pale pink and there's lots of crackling.

1 small leg pork, pumped and skin scored for crackling
little cooking salt

When ordering from the butcher, ask him to pump the leg but to leave it in the pickle for 1-2 hours (no more). Place meat into a baking dish skin side up, rub skin with just a little salt, and bake in a moderately slow oven allowing about 25-30 minutes per 500 g (1 lb). To crisp crackling, increase oven temperature to full blast during last ½ hour or so.

This is delicious served hot or cold. Serve with lots of homemade apple sauce (the recipe is on page 71).

Note: The loin of pork either with or without the bone is also very successful cooked this way.

FRIED RICE

Fried rice is as much part of our everyday eating in Australia now as steak and eggs were a decade ago.
Pine nuts, browned lightly in a little butter or oil, make an interesting addition to the rice. Add just before serving.

500 g (1 lb) shortgrain calrose rice
2 eggs, beaten
½ bunch shallots
2 tablespoons peanut oil
3 bacon rashers, chopped, or piece Chinese barbecued pork, sliced
½ teaspoon green ginger, grated
½ cup frozen peas (optional)
½ level teaspoon salt (or to taste)
few drops of sesame oil
2 or 3 teaspoons soy sauce
250 g (½ lb) small peeled prawns

Boil the rice the day before and spread out onto a tray. Cover lightly then store in refrigerator. Put a few drops of oil in the bottom of a frying pan or wok and fry eggs in a thin pancake. Break up with a fork and remove to a plate and reserve. Trim shallots, chop white portion and reserve the green. Heat oil in wok or frypan and fry bacon or babecued pork for a few minutes, then push to one side and fry chopped shallots and ginger. Add rice and toss together, fry quickly, tossing or stirring from time to time so that rice is well heated and coated with oil. Add peas and allow to heat through, then add cooked egg, salt, sesame oil and soy. If the rice seems a little dry, add a few drops of water as this has the effect of 'plumping' the rice. Add prawns and heat through. Slice the green part of the shallots and toss through, reserving some to sprinkle on top when serving.

HAM AND RICE SALAD

The secret of success with this salad is to use a good classic mayonnaise. A good salad to serve around Christmas time when there's an abundance of thick juicy ham chunks.

1½ cups raw rice (calrose short grain is best for this recipe)
2 firm ripe tomatoes
approximately 500 g (1 lb) ham, cut into chunks
approximately 4 heaped tablespoons mayonnaise
crisp lettuce leaves
black olives

Cook rice in boiling salted water until just tender. Rinse, drain and cool. Cut tomatoes into halves, squeeze out seeds gently, then cut the flesh into tiny cubes (the juicy seeds would break down the mayonnaise). Cut ham into chunky cubes. Put rice into a mixing bowl and add sufficient mayonnaise to make a moist mixture, then stir through the tomato and ham. Season to taste with salt and pepper. Put a bed of crisp lettuce leaves onto a plate (a compote or glass cake stand looks pretty). Pile the rice salad up in a little mountain and dot with shiny black olives.

RICE SALAD WITH MUSHROOMS

Combine the rice salad with mushroom salad (the recipe is on page 107) just before serving and toss together lightly. Pile into a lettuce-lined bowl and scatter over the olives.

CRISPY CHICKEN IN MANGO SAUCE

4 chicken fillets
1 level tablespoon plain flour
1 egg, beaten
dry breadcrumbs (or mixture
dry breadcrumbs and finely
chopped blanched almonds)
60 g (2 oz) butter for frying
1 mango
juice of 1 orange
pinch of chilli powder or dash
of sweet chilli sauce

Dust chicken fillets lightly with flour, then dip into beaten egg and straight into crumbs, or mixture of crumbs and almonds. Press on firmly. Put butter into a frying pan and melt gently, then add chicken fillets. Continue to cook over a fairly low heat (crumbs tend to burn easily, especially with almonds) until the chicken is cooked and coating is golden both sides, about 10 minutes (try not to overcook, chicken should be still juicy). Alternatively, if entertaining and unable to watch carefully, simply brown lightly in butter then transfer to a baking dish, and cook in a moderate oven for about 20 minutes. Puree flesh of mango in a food processor or blender, adding juice to thin to desired consistency. Spike with little chilli. Heat gently in a separate pan and serve as a sauce *under* the chicken on the plate. Serves 4.

CHICKEN CASSEROLE

2.5 kg (5 lb) chicken pieces
3 level tablespoons plain flour
90 g (3 oz) butter
2-3 bacon rashers
2 onions, peeled and sliced
2 fat cloves garlic, crushed
1½ cups dry white wine
1-2 tablespoons port
½ level teaspoon salt
pepper to taste
good pinch of dried tarragon
or thyme
1 bay leaf
250 g button mushrooms,
sliced
extra 30 g (1 oz) butter
2 tablespoons cream (optional)
fresh parsley, chopped

Dust chicken pieces in flour. Brown slowly in butter in a large frying pan. Remove chicken to a casserole. Chop bacon and add to pan, when fat starts to sizzle, fry onion and garlic. Cook well then add to chicken with wine, port, herbs, salt and pepper. Cover tightly and cook in a moderate oven for 1-1¼ hours. Meanwhile, sauté mushrooms in little extra butter and stir through the casserole with cream. Heat through and serve sprinkled with parsley. Serves 8.

CHICKEN IN GREEN PEPPERCORN SAUCE

This a most successful dish that everyone seems to love.

4 single chicken fillets
1 level tablespoon plain flour
30 g (1 oz) butter
1 tablespoon port
½ cup dry white wine
½ cup water
1 level tablespoon green peppercorns (½ small can)
pinch of salt
2 tablespoons cream

Dust chicken fillets lightly with flour. Melt butter in a frying pan and add chicken fillets. Fry gently until light golden on both sides. Add port, white wine, water, green peppercorns and tiny pinch of salt. Simmer gently for approximately 10 minutes or until the chicken is tender. Remove chicken to hot serving plates. Boil the sauce rapidly to reduce it to a shiny glaze, add cream, heat through, then pour over the chicken and serve. Serves 4.

Opposite: Chicken in green peppercorn sauce.

CHICKEN BREASTS IN FRESH TOMATO SAUCE

A quick little dinner that's easy to prepare when entertaining mid-week. Chicken supremes are chicken breasts with the first joint of the wing attached and bone removed but skin attached.

6 chicken fillets or chicken supremes
1 small onion, peeled and sliced
1 large clove garlic, crushed
1 tablespoon each butter and olive oil
1 level tablespoon plain flour
250 g (½ lb) button mushrooms, sliced
extra 30 g (1 oz) butter
3 large ripe tomatoes, skinned
1 tablespoon port
1 cup water
¼ cup white wine
1 stick celery finely chopped
½ level teaspoon dried oregano
sprig rosemary or pinch dried rosemary
500 g (1 lb) fresh fettuccine noodles (or 375 g dried fettuccine)
dob butter, olive oil, grated parmesan or romano cheese
chopped parsley to garnish

Fry onion and garlic in oil and butter until soft, allowing 5-10 minutes slow cooking to develop flavour. Move onions to one side of pan and increase heat. Fry floured chicken until golden both sides. Remove chicken to a plate. Add extra butter to frying pan and mix mushrooms with onions and oil left in pan. Fry few minutes then add chopped tomatoes, port, water, wine and celery. Season with salt, pepper and herbs. Simmer for five minutes to develop a rich tomato sauce. Place chicken on top of sauce. Cover with a lid or foil and simmer for about 15 minutes or until the chicken is tender.

Serve with freshly cooked fettuccine tossed in butter and olive oil with freshly ground black pepper and sprinkled with cheese. Garnish with chopped fresh parlsey. Accompany with a green salad. Serves 6.

EASY ROAST CHICKEN

This is a simple recipe when you don't have time to cook. Quantities could be increased to cater for a crowd. The chicken turns the most beautiful golden colour and the soup, wine and chicken juices make a delicious smooth gravy.

1½ kg (3 lb) chicken pieces
1 heaped tablespoon butter
1 can cream of chicken soup
½ cup dry white wine
pinch of dried thyme

Put chicken pieces into a baking tray in a single layer. Dot with butter. Roast uncovered in a moderately hot oven for ½ hour. Mix soup, wine and thyme and pour over chicken. Bake a further ¾ hour. The skin takes on a most beautiful golden colour and the chicken is always tender and juicy. Remove the chicken from the baking dish onto warmed serving plates. Pour gravy in dish into a jug, skim away any excess butter. Pour gravy over chicken and serve hot. Serves 6.

MASTERING THE ART OF A PERFECT BAKED DINNER
ROAST LAMB

A baked dinner is one of the easiest meals to prepare, but understandably it seems to worry young and inexperienced cooks, especially at the last minute. There's the gravy to make, the meat to carve and it's often hard to judge the cooking time of meat and vegetables so that they're all ready together.

Rub a little salt and pepper into a leg of lamb (2 kg or 4 lb) and place into a baking dish.

Bake in a hot oven for about 2 hours (more or less according to taste, but traditionally Australian roast lamb is not served underdone).

Peeled vegetables (chunks of pumpkin, sweet potato and halved or quartered potatoes) are placed around the meat during last ½-¾ hour of cooking.

When the meat is cooked, remove from oven and stand for 15-20 minutes before carving. The vegetables and fat should be transfered to another baking tray and crisped in the oven which has been turned to high (see also hints on crispy baked potatoes on page 108).

Carve the meat and serve with gravy and mint sauce and baked vegetables and sweet young green peas.

Gravy: Unthickened gravy is easier to make, simply pour off excess fat in the dish, swill out baking dish with water and pour into a cup. Add ice cubes to bring fat to the surface, then return meat juices (minus fat) to baking dish and reheat. Season with salt and pepper to taste.

Thickened gravy: Pour off all but 1 or 2 tablespoons fat from the baking dish, sprinkle over 1 level tablespoon plain flour and make a roux. Brown lightly. Add sufficient water to make a thin gravy and season with salt and pepper and pour into a gravy dish.

MINT SAUCE

2 level tablespoons fresh mint, chopped
1 tablespoon boiling water
¼ cup brown or white vinegar
1-1½ level tablespoons sugar
pinch of salt and pepper

Put chopped mint into a small bowl. Pour over boiling water (this sets the colour). Add remaining ingredients. Stand for 1 hour before using.

ROAST DUCK

If cooking duck for the first time be warned that, unlike chicken, an average sized duck (size 16) will serve 2 people or 3 at the most.

To prepare for cooking: Remove any giblets and the neck. Cut off the wing tips and save these to make a rich broth for the gravy. Pour boiling water into the cavity to rinse out then fill this cavity with chopped Granny Smith apples to keep the flesh moist. Rub the skin well with salt and, for a good shape, tie the legs close to the body with string. Bake breast side up in a baking dish for about 2 hours. Simmer reserved giblets, neck, etc. with a bouquet garni and a few slices onion in sufficient water to cover. Strain, skim off any fat and reserve for gravy.

Gravy: Remove cooked ducks from pan and before pouring off the duck fat, boil drippings in a baking dish over high heat to drive off excess liquid. Pour off all but 1 tablespoon fat then sprinkle this with 1 level tablespoon plain flour to make a roux. Add strained duck broth and stir until thickened, thinning if necessary with water. Season with salt and pepper.

Orange sauce: Boil finest shreds of orange peel in water with a pinch of sugar until tender. Add these with juice of 1 orange and ½ lemon. Taste and adjust flavours. A tablespoon red currant jelly adds a richness to the flavour.

No panic system: Ducks, I've discovered over the years, can be unpredictible. The safest plan when entertaining is to allow a little extra time by cooking the ducks half an hour or so earlier than you plan to serve them. That way, if they're not tender, the portions could be slipped back into the gravy or sauce and returned to the oven for extra cooking (many Australians do not like rare duck).

ROAST BEEF (WING RIB)

3 kg (6 lb) wing rib
salt and pepper
Yorkshire pudding

Ask the butcher to saw through the chine bone (this makes the carving easier).

Sprinkle a little salt and freshly ground pepper onto the fat layer and score skin for an attractive presentation at the table. Place into a baking dish, fat side up. The ribs will form a natural trivet in the bottom of the dish. Roast in a hot oven for 1-1¼ hours for beef that is pink or slightly rare in the centre. For well done beef which is slightly pink in the centre, allow 10 minutes extra. Remove from oven and rest in a warm place for 15 minutes before carving. Serve with Yorkshire pudding and an unthickened gravy made with meat juices from the baking dish, skimmed free of all fat and diluted with a little water and a tiny dash of red wine. Serves 6-8.

YORKSHIRE PUDDING

1 cup plain flour
½ level teaspoon salt
2 eggs
½ cup milk
½ cup water
4 tablespoons beef dripping (saved from previous roasts)
1 set patty tins or muffin tins

Make a batter with the flour, salt, eggs and milk, beating well until smooth then beat in the water. Refrigerate until ready to cook and beat again just before using. Heat patty or muffin tins in a hot oven with 1 teaspoon dripping in each one. When dripping is smoking hot, pour in the

SAUSAGE ROLLS

Homemade sausage rolls are still a popular party snack. Here's a good recipe.

1 kg (2 lb) good quality sausage mince
1 onion, peeled and finely chopped
1 tablespoon butter
1 clove garlic, crushed
¼ cup parsley, chopped
good pinch of dried thyme
½ level teaspoon salt
freshly ground black pepper
2 large eggs
3 sheets ready rolled puff pastry
1 small egg for glazing
Swiss roll tin (or baking tray with sides to contain any melted fat from the sausage mince)

Sauté onion in butter until soft. Put into a mixing bowl and add sausage mince, garlic, herbs, seasonings and eggs. Mix thoroughly. Cut each pastry sheet into halves. Pile the sausage mince down the centre of each strip and brush edges of pastry with beaten egg. Bring pastry over the meat, overlapping slightly. Place (join underneath) onto greased baking tray. Make a few steam vents and with a small sharp knife. Brush with beaten egg. Bake in a hot oven for about 25 minutes. Cut across into individual pieces. Serve hot. Makes about 3 dozen.

Note: For a change from the traditional tomato sauce, try serving with a dipping sauce of sweet and sour (there are many good quality bottled sweet and sour sauces available in Chinese grocery shops).

FILLET OF BEEF IN GREEN PEPPERCORN SAUCE

2 whole eye fillets
white string
1 tablespoon butter
1½-2 cups jellied beef stock,
prepared the day before
2 tablespoons port
½ level teaspoon dried
tarragon leaves
1 small can (55 g) green
peppercorns (approx 2 level
tablespoons)
fresh parsley for serving,
chopped

Remove excess fat from fillets. Slip a small vegetable knife under the thin white membrane on the fillet and strip it away. Tie each fillet in two or three places with white string so they keep their shape. Heat butter in a frying pan and, when just turning golden brown, add the fillets. Turn carefully with a couple of spoons to brown well on all sides. Put into a small baking dish and bake in a hot oven for 20-30 minutes (depending on the thickness of the meat and how rare you prefer). Allow to stand for 5 minutes before carving. While the meat is cooking prepare the sauce. Melt the jellied beef stock in a frying pan. Add port, tarragon and well drained green peppercorns. Taste, adjust seasonings. Remove string from beef, cut into thick slices and arrange on a meat dish. Spoon over the luscious green peppercorn sauce and sprinkle with parsley. Serve with plain boiled peeled new potatoes or a big bowl of fluffy creamed potato and fresh young beans. Serves 6-8, depending on the size of the fillets.

JELLIED BEEF STOCK

Make up the recipe for rich beef stock (see page 17). Strain and refrigerate overnight and skim away all fat. Put the stock into a big pot and boil with the lid off until reduced to about 2 cups. Pour into a bowl and refrigerate. It will set to a very firm jelly.

FILLET STEAK WITH OYSTER SAUCE

Oyster sauce with steak was a popular dish with Irish settlers back in the early days of the colony.

1 kg (2 lb) fillet steak
2 level tablespoons butter
2 level tablespoons plain flour
1½ cups milk
salt and pepper
good pinch of cayenne
squeeze of lemon juice
2 tablespoons cream
2 dozen oysters

Melt butter, add flour to form a roux and cook without browning for a minute or so. Add milk and stir until sauce boils and thickens. Beat well. Season to taste, and enrich with the cream. Add oysters just before serving and simply allow to heat through. Do not boil or they will toughen. Serve over cooked fillet steaks or sliced whole fillet. Serves 4-6.

BEARNAISE SAUCE

My son David adores this sauce. Every birthday dinner for the last ten years or more he has requested tournedos and bearnaise sauce, so David, this is for you.

Note: When entertaining the last minute reheating of the sauce can be a risky business unless very careful. I suggest, especially if making it for the first time, that the sauce be spooned into a dish and kept at room temperature. Allow guests to spoon over meat at the table.

1 level tablespoon shallot bulbs, finely chopped
a few whole peppercorns
6 tablespoons vinegar (½ brown and ½ white or tarragon)
good pinch of dried tarragon
4 egg yolks
185 g (6 oz) butter, melted or cut into tiny squares (room temperature)
1 teaspoon parsley or chervil, very finely chopped (optional)

Put shallots, peppercorns, vinegars and tarragon into a small saucepan and simmer over a very low heat until reduced to half (if accidentally the vinegar reduces too much, replace with water). Strain into a small heatproof basin (there should be 3 tablespoons).

Add egg yolks and whisk well. Place over gentle simmering water and beat until yolks start to thicken (use wire whisk or small wooden spoon). Add the butter gradually, drop by drop or one square at a time, beating all the time. After half the butter has been added the critical time is over and it can be added a little faster. Remove from the heat and stir in herbs and salt.

Serve at room temperature (or reheated in a warm water bath) over hot roasted beef or steaks. Good also with chicken and tiny new potatoes or with baby lamb chops.

BEEFSTEAK PUDDING

Tender meat steamed in its own juices topped with a light suet crust. Such simple flavour, but that's the secret of grandma's beefsteak pudding! There's no place for garlic or tomato paste in this recipe.

750 g (1½ lb) bladebone steak
1 onion
½ level teaspoon salt (or to taste)
lots of freshly ground black pepper
¾ cup water

SUET PASTE
1 cup SR flour
60 g (2 oz) coarsely grated suet (1 cup, lightly filled)
¼ level teaspoon salt
approximately ½ cup water

Trim meat, chop into small cubes and put into a small pudding basin (a 6 cup aluminium basin with a clip lid is ideal for this recipe). Chop onion very finely, mix in with the meat, then add salt, pepper and water.
Sift flour and salt into a basin, mix suet through lightly, coating well with flour. Mix into a soft scone consistency with water, then remove from basin and knead very lightly. Pat out into a thick circle to fit the top of the pudding basin. Place on top of meat, making sure that there is room to rise (about 2.5 cm or 1 inch). Cover with a circle of greased gladbake or greaseproof, then clip on the lid or cover with two sheets of foil, tied securely. Lower into a saucepan with boiling water coming half way up the sides of the basin. Cover pot and simmer for 3 hours, replacing boiling water as necessary. Serves 4.
Note: 1 or 2 finely chopped lamb's kidneys or a couple of rashers of finely chopped bacon could be added if desired.

AUSTRALIAN MEAT PIE

This is a good recipe for one of our traditional, and most famous, dishes. The pastry is crumbly and delicious, and can be made in the food processor. The recipe is on page 84.

1 ox kidney (optional)
juice of ½ lemon
3 bacon rashers, chopped
2 onions, peeled and sliced
1.5-2 kg (3-4 lb) chuck steak, trimmed and chopped into small cubes
2 cups water
½ teaspoon black pepper
½-1 level teaspoon salt
few sprigs of fresh thyme or ½ level teaspoon dried thyme
1 stick celery, finely chopped
3 tablespoons plain flour
1 recipe shortcrust pastry

Soak the kidney in a little water with lemon juice for ½ hour to remove any strong flavour. Fry chopped bacon in a large heavy based saucepan, and when the fat starts to sizzle add the onion. Fry over a low heat until the onion is soft. Add chopped steak and finely chopped kidney. Pour in water and season with pepper, salt and thyme, then add the celery. Cover and simmer gently for about 1½ hours. Smooth out the flour with a little extra cold water, then stir this into the meat. Stir over the heat until thick. Pour into a deep pie dish of 2 litre (8 cups) capacity. If you own a pie funnel, place in the centre of the meat (you could substitute an upturned egg cup). Roll out the pastry, cut a few strips for a collar. Place these on the wet rim of the pie dish and brush with milk or beaten egg. Lift remaining pastry onto a rolling pin and place on top of the pie. Trim

Opposite: Australian meat pie.

edges with a knife. Press edges together with a fork to seal. Make a few steam holes. Glaze with beaten egg or milk and bake in a hot oven for 30-40 minutes. Serves 6-8.

SHORTCRUST PASTRY

¾ cup plain flour
¾ cup SR flour
pinch of salt
100 g (3½ oz) cooking margarine or butter
3 tablespoons cold water
1 teaspoon lemon juice

Place flours and salt into a mixing bowl, rub in margarine with fingertips and mix into a dough with water and lemon juice. Turn out onto a lightly floured surface and knead lightly with little flour. Rest for 20 minutes before rolling.

To make in food processor: Use chilled butter cut into small chunks. Place flours, salt and butter into food processor and process for a few seconds to cut in the butter. Add water and juice, then process only long enough for the mixture to start to form a dough. Do not overmix. Turn out and knead lightly and rest as above before rolling.

SAVOURY POCKET STEAK (SWISS STEAK)

Pocket steak has an onion filling and is baked slowly with vegetables in a fresh tomato sauce.

1 double thick slice bladebone or topside steak (ask butcher to cut a pocket), approx 750 g (1½ lb)
2 medium sized onions, peeled and sliced

1 tablespoon butter
3 level tablespoons plain
flour
salt and pepper
1 level tablespoon dry
mustard
1 heaped tablespoon butter
or bacon drippings
3 large ripe tomatoes,
peeled and sliced
1 large carrot, peeled and
sliced
1 stick celery, chopped
1 tablespoon Worcestershire
sauce
½ cup hot water

Fry onions in butter until soft and glossy, then spoon into pocket of the steak. Mix flour, salt, pepper and mustard together on a plate. Coat steak well with flour mixture. Heat butter or bacon drippings in a frying pan. Add steak and brown well on both sides. Transfer the steak to a shallow casserole. Cover with sliced tomatoes, then add vegetables, Worcestershire sauce and water. Add a good pinch of salt and grind in some black pepper. Cover casserole and bake in a moderate oven for 1½-2 hours. Cut steak into four and serve with the vegetables and delicious cooking broth. Accompany with fluffy mashed potatoes and fresh bread and butter plus boiled whole green beans or sweet young peas. Serves 4.

BEEF BURGUNDY

Rich and full of flavour, this is a good choice for casual entertaining during winter.

2 streaky bacon rashers
1 large onion, peeled and chopped
1 fat clove garlic, crushed
1½ kg (3 lb) chuck steak (best steak to use as it doesn't become stringy)
2 level tablespoons plain flour
30 g (1 oz) butter
½ cup water
1 stick celery, finely diced
1½ cups burgundy or dry red wine
2 tablespoons port (optional)
1 rounded tablespoon tomato paste
1 bay leaf
½ level teaspoon dried thyme leaves
pinch of ground nutmeg
freshly ground black pepper
½ level teaspoon salt (or to taste)
250 g (½ lb) mushrooms
½ cup parsley, chopped

Chop bacon and put into a large frying pan. Fry gently until fat sizzles, move to one side of pan and add sliced onion and crushed garlic. Sauté for 5 minutes, then remove to a casserole dish. Trim chuck steak and cut into fairly large pieces. Roll in flour. Add butter to frying pan, brown meat, then add to the casserole. Rinse out pan with water, pour over meat then add celery, wine, port, tomato paste, herbs and seasonings. Push meat down into liquid, adding a little extra water if necessary to cover meat. Cover with lid and cook in a very slow oven for 3 hours. Slice mushrooms and sauté quickly in little extra butter and stir through beef. Serve sprinkled with chopped parsley. Have a big dish of steaming hot boiled new potatoes and lots of hot crusty bread to mop up luscious gravy. A plain green salad works well as accompaniment but if it's really chilly try serving a dish of sweet young green peas (they're especially sweet and tender in winter). Serves 6-8.

HUNGARIAN GOULASH

Goulash doesn't seem to be as popular in Australia just at the moment but ten years ago it was very 'in'. Along with chicken paprika and beef stroganoff, it was all part of the 'continental cooking' craze we were experiencing at the time.

1 kg (2 lb) bladebone steak
2 level tablespoons plain flour
1 heaped tablespoon butter
1 onion, peeled and sliced
500 g (1 lb) cooking tomatoes
1 level tablespoon paprika
1½ cups water
½ level teaspoon salt
500 g (1 lb) potatoes
fresh parsley, chopped

Trim meat, cut into cubes and roll in the flour. Melt butter in a large heavy based saucepan, fry onions for few minutes, then add floured meat. Stir around over fairly high heat to seal the meat, then add chopped tomatoes, paprika, water and salt. Cover and simmer very gently for 1¼-1½ hours.
Peel and slice potatoes, add to meat with an extra cup of water. Cover and simmer gently for a further 15 minutes. Watch that the meat does not catch on the bottom of the pan at this stage. Sprinkle with parsley. Serves 4-5.

BEEF AND CASHEWS

500 g (1 lb) tender steak
(scotch fillet, fillet or rump)
oil to deep fry beef

COATING MIXTURE
1 egg (could use just egg white)
1 level tablespoon cornflour
pinch of sugar
few drops of sesame oil
1 teaspoon soy sauce

SAUCE
1 onion, peeled and cut into
eighths from stem to base
1 fat clove garlic, crushed
1 teaspoon green
ginger, grated
2 sticks celery, sliced
½ cup frozen peas
1 cup water
1 small chicken cube
1 tablespoon oyster sauce
1 teaspoon soy sauce
1 level tablespoon cornflour
mixed with little extra water
½ cup unsalted cashews, fried
until golden in little oil
few shallot tops, sliced

Slice beef diagonally into thin bite sized pieces. Put into a bowl with ingredients for the coating mixture. Mix around well. Heat oil in a wok. Add beef pieces (not all at once or they'll cook in a clump). Seal quickly then remove beef to a bowl. Cover to keep warm. Empty all but 1 tablespoon oil from wok. Add onion, garlic and ginger. Stir fry quickly, then add celery, peas, water, chicken cube and sauces.

Bring to boil. Thicken with blended cornflour then return beef. Mix well, adjust seasonings and consistency. Serve scattered with crispy fried cashews and sliced shallot tops. Serve with plain boiled rice. Serves 4.

STEAK DIANE

Romanos restaurant in Sydney introduced Steak Diane to Australia when their head waiter, Toni Clerici, brought the recipe with him from the Dorchester in England. Although there have been many variations since, here is the original recipe.

2 thick fillet steaks
freshly ground black pepper
60 g (2 oz) butter
1 tablespoon Worcestershire sauce
1 large clove garlic, crushed
2 tablespoons parsley, chopped
pinch of salt

Pound the steaks with a meat mallet or rolling pin (wet the mallet or rolling pin first, so it doesn't stick to the meat or cover the meat with plastic). The steaks should be flattened into thin steaks about the size of a bread and butter plate. Season meat with freshly ground pepper. Heat butter in a large frying pan and when very hot and just starting to colour add the steaks. Cook over a very high heat for one minute on each side. Add Worcestershire sauce, garlic, chopped parsley and tiny pinch of salt. Serve immediately. Serves 2.

Variations: If the pungent flavour of the Worcestershire sauce is too strong for your palate, try softening the sauce with a little cream. Another variation that I find works particularly well with young palates is to reduce the Worcestershire sauce and add just a dash of tomato sauce, thin out the sauce with a tablespoon or so of water, then finish with a little cream.

CURRY

*The addition of peanuts
makes a subtle difference
to this curry.
This curry is best made
the day before. Serve with
boiled rice, poppadums
and side dishes.*

*1.5 kg (3 lb) chuck steak or
1 leg lamb, boned
60 g (2 oz) butter or ghee
1 large onion, sliced
2 large cloves garlic, peeled
and crushed
1 heaped teaspoon green
ginger, grated
3 teaspoons ground coriander
1 teaspoon ground cummin
1 teaspoon turmeric
6 cardamon pods
(or ¼ teaspoon cardamon seeds)
1 cinnamon stick
½ cup roasted peanuts,
finely chopped
3-4 cups water
juice of 1 big lemon
1-2 ripe tomatoes, peeled
and chopped
1 chilli, finely chopped
2 level tablespoons Jimmy's
Satay Sauce (optional)
60 g (2 oz) compressed coconut
cream
1 tablespoon Malaysian mild
chilli sauce (optional)
1 level teaspoon salt
freshly ground black pepper*

Trim meat and cut into large cubes. Melt butter or ghee in
a large frying pan and sauté onion gently for about 10
minutes. Add garlic, ginger and curry spices and fry a few
minutes longer. Add meat cubes and brown well on all
sides. Transfer to a heavy based saucepan and add

90

remaining ingredients. Simmer gently, allowing ¾-1 hour if using lamb and 1¼-1½ hours if using the chuck steak. Watch that it doesn't catch on the bottom as the liquid evaporates.

APPLE SAMBAL

3 large Granny Smith apples
1 large lemon, juiced
1 chilli, finely chopped
1 small white onion, peeled
and very finely chopped
½ cup desiccated coconut
pinch each of salt and sugar

Cut peeled apples into tiny dice. Put into a bowl and add lemon juice. Toss well to coat apple (this stops discolouration). Add chopped chilli and onion. Soften coconut in a little warm water then squeeze dry. Sprinkle over the apples. Season with salt and a tiny pinch of sugar.

TOMATO SAMBAL

2-3 firm ripe tomatoes
2 small white onions, peeled
and finely sliced
1 level teaspoon sugar
salt and pepper to taste
½ cup vinegar
juice of 1 lemon
fresh mint, chopped

Slice tomatoes and put into a shallow dish. Add the onion, sugar, salt, pepper, vinegar and stand for ½ hour, then add fresh lemon juice and sprinkle with mint.

CUCUMBER SALAD

Peel cucumbers and cut into strips, discarding the seeds. Put into a dish and sprinkle with salt. Stand ½ hour or so then drain away excess liquid. Stir through natural yoghurt or light sour cream and sprinkle with chopped chives.

SHEPHERD'S PIE

My children adore this shepherd's pie, but I must confess that before I owned a food processor, I didn't make it very often (putting the lamb through the old mincer attached to the kitchen table was much more fun for the children of the house than the cook).

750 g (1½ lb) potatoes, peeled
2-3 cups minced left-over roast lamb
1 onion, peeled and sliced
30 g (1 oz) butter
1 large carrot, grated
1 small fresh tomato, chopped
¼ cup celery, very finely chopped (optional)
few shakes of Worcestershire sauce
½ cup tomato sauce
1-2 tablespoons water
good pinch of salt
lots of freshly ground black pepper
extra 30 g (1 oz) butter, melted

Boil potatoes in a covered saucepan. Place minced lamb in a bowl. Sauté onion in butter until soft and add to the lamb with the carrot, tomato, celery, sauces and water. Season with salt and pepper. Spread into a greased pie dish. Drain and mash potatoes. Add the butter, salt and pepper, and beat well. The mixture will be fairly dry but that is the secret of a crispy topping. Pile this potato over the lamb and rough with a fork. Brush with a little additional butter and bake in a hot oven for about 45 minutes. Serves 4-5.

SPAGHETTI BOLOGNAISE

1 large onion, peeled and sliced
30 g (1 oz) butter
500 g (1 lb) hamburger mince
2 cloves garlic, crushed
1 teaspoon dried basil
½ level teaspoon dried oregano
1 bay leaf
1 tablespoon fresh parsley,
chopped
2 level tablespoons tomato
paste
1 can whole peeled tomatoes
½ cup red or white wine
1 cup water
125 g (¼ lb) mushrooms,
finely sliced
250 g (½ lb) spaghetti (more if
fresh)
grated cheese

Melt butter in a large saucepan and fry onion until soft. Add meat and brown lightly, then add garlic, herbs, tomato paste, tomatoes, wine, and water. Cover and simmer for 1 hour, adding the mushrooms for the last 10 minutes. The sauce should be rich and thick. Boil rapidly to reduce if necessary. Serve over hot spaghetti and sprinkle with grated cheese. Serves 4-6.

VEGETABLES AND VEGETARIAN DISHES

The variety of vegetables increases every year in Australia and our shops are filled with a myriad of choices. The general swing to eating more vegetables and less meat is evident and recipes for vegetarian foods are more popular than ever before.

Carrots in golden egg sauce, page 96.

95

CARROTS IN GOLDEN EGG SAUCE

750 g (1 ½ lb) young carrots,
peeled
1 level teaspoon sugar
tiny pinch of salt (optional)
3 egg yolks
¾ cup cream
2 teaspoons lemon juice
1 tablespoon chives or parsley,
chopped

Cut carrots lengthways into quarters, and then across into finger lengths. Boil in a heavy based saucepan with sugar, a tiny pinch of salt and enough water to barely cover. Cook, covered, for 15 minutes or until tender. Drain away all but 1 tablespoon of the liquid. Mix yolks, cream and lemon juice together. Reduce heat under the saucepan containing carrots and pour in the cream mixture. Stir gently over a low heat until the sauce just starts to thicken into a very smooth and shiny sauce. Be careful not to overcook or the eggs will scramble. Serve immediately sprinkled with herbs. Serves 6.

LITTLE CORN CAKES

Serve as a vegetable accompaniment or with bacon for brunch.

⅔ cup plain flour
good pinch of salt
½ level teaspoon ground nutmeg
2 eggs
1 cup milk
2 tablespoons melted butter
1 can 440 g (14 oz) whole kernel corn, drained
1 tablespoon chives or parsley, finely chopped
freshly ground black pepper

Preheat oven to hottest temperature. Sift flour, salt and nutmeg into a mixing bowl and add eggs, milk and melted butter. Add well drained corn and a little freshly ground black pepper. Mix together, then stir in chopped chives or parsley. Brush aluminium patty tins well with butter and almost fill each tin with the mixture. Use approximately 2 tablespoons for filling. Bake in a very hot oven for 15-20 minutes. Makes about 18-20.

HUMMUS BI TAHINI

A Lebanese dip to serve with flat bread.

125 g (4 oz) chick peas
4-5 cloves garlic
½ cup lemon juice
½ cup tahini (sesame butter)
salt to taste
a few tablespoons oil
paprika and parsley for garnish
lebanese bread for serving

Soak chick peas in water overnight. Rinse and cover with clean water and boil for about two hours or until tender (or in a pressure cooker 20 minutes). Drain, saving some of the cooking liquid. Save three whole peas for garnish and purée the remainder in a food processor or blender or use a mouli mill. Add some of the liquid to thin down, then add crushed garlic, lemon juice and tahini. Beat well together and season with salt to taste. Thin down with a tablespoon or so of oil and cooking liquid. Put into a bowl, spoon over oil and cover tightly with plastic. Refrigerate until ready to serve. Garnish with whole chick peas, a sprig of Italian parsley and a sprinkle of paprika. Serve as a dip with Lebanese bread cut into triangles.

SPINACH SALAD

1 bunch English spinach or
silverbeet
1 small mild flavoured white
onion
1 tablespoon toasted sesame
seeds
1 clove garlic, crushed
½ level teaspoon French
mustard
1 tablespoon lemon juice
3 tablespoons salad oil
2 bacon rashers, cooked and
crumbled
2 tablespoons toasted pine
nuts
2 eggs, softly scrambled

Wash spinach very well, strip away white stems. When using English spinach, take the youngest leaves and tear into bite sized pieces, but if using silverbeet, shred finely. Place the leaves into a salad bowl and add paper thin slices of onion and sesame seeds. Make a dressing with crushed garlic, mustard, oil and lemon, and shake well. Pour over spinach and toss well. Sprinkle with bacon, pine nuts and egg. Serves 6-8.

SPINACH PIE

2 bunches silverbeet
1 cup shallots, chopped
2 tablespoons oil or butter
1 tablespoon parsley, chopped
1 tablespoon mint or dill,
chopped
250 g (8 oz) feta cheese
5 eggs
good pinch of nutmeg
salt to taste
freshly ground black pepper
½ packet filo pastry
½-¾ cup melted butter

Wash spinach in two or three changes of cold water. Shred leaves finely, discarding white stems. Heat oil or butter in a large saucepan and fry shallots for a few minutes. Add spinach, cover and cook for about 5 minutes, shaking the pot from time to time for even cooking. Remove lid, press spinach down with potato masher then drain away as much liquid as possible. Place spinach into a bowl to cool. When cool, add herbs, feta, beaten eggs and seasonings and mix together well.

Unwrap filo pastry and place between two dry teatowels with an additional damp teatowel (well wrung out) over the top. Line a lamington tin with 6 layers of filo, brushing each layer with butter. Fill with spinach mixture then cover with another 6 layers of the buttered filo pastry. Press down firmly and trim away excess pastry with a sharp knife. Bake in a moderate oven for ¾-1 hour. Stand 5 minutes before cutting. Serve with a crispy green salad. Serves 6.
Note: The filling is also delicious baked in little ramekins without the pastry and with a little grated cheese on top.

CHOKOS

Choko vines rambling over backyard fences feature in many an Australian garden. Choko addicts say the only way to eat them is when they are very tiny and young, simply boiled in a little water and dressed with a big dob of butter and lots of freshly ground pepper. Here are some other ways to enjoy their unique and delicate flavour.

Peel (best to do this under running water), remove core and cut chokos into large cubes. Cook in a heavy saucepan with a little olive oil and sufficient water to prevent sticking. Add a little crushed garlic. Cover and braise over a medium heat for about 10 minutes, tossing from time to time. A cubed potato could be added for variety. Add a little chopped fresh basil or mint towards the end of the cooking time.

Use only very young and tender chokos for this next recipe. Peel chokos and slice finely. Remove core if you wish but when young it can also be used (some say it's the best part). Stir fry quickly in butter with finely chopped bacon and a little crushed garlic. Pour in equal quantities of cream and water, sufficient to create a sauce. Simmer gently until chokos are crispy tender and the cream mixture has reduced to a sauce. Sprinkle with chopped chives.

BEETROOT

Beetroot is making a comeback in Australia at the moment. Once only reserved for salads it is now taking its rightful place as a vegetable accompaniment. We are seeing it used in Nouvelle Cuisine-style presentations – simply boiled then fanned onto the plate. It is also being used raw in whispy thin shreds to add a splash of brilliant red to pretty little first course salads.

Home gardeners will know the pleasure of harvesting baby beets to serve whole. (I am very spoilt here, my sister Jenny grows them especially for me.)

BOILED BEETROOT

Wash beetroot, try not to damage the skins and cut away leaves, leaving a 3 cm (1½ inches) stem (this stops the beets 'bleeding' and losing colour). Boil in water to cover for 1-1½ hours (baby beets will take only about 30 minutes). When cooked, drain and plunge into cold water then slip away the skins. Slice if large and toss in a little melted butter to reheat. Serve hot sprinkled with chopped chives.

BEETROOT PICKLE

Slice beetroot into a bowl. Sprinkle each layer with a little sugar and a tiny pinch of nutmeg, pepper and salt. Pour over a mixture of equal quantities of brown vinegar and water. Store in refrigerator.

BAKED BEETROOT

Wash beetroots, do not peel and leave a 3 cm (1½ inches) stem. Put into a casserole containing a little water and bake in a moderate oven for about 2 hours, adding extra hot water as necessary if it evaporates away. When cooked, slip away the skins and slice. Dress with a dob of butter and good squeeze lemon juice.

RAW BEETROOT

Peel beetroot and grate coarsely or cut into fine julienne strips. Add to salads.

VEGETABLE SPAGHETTI

A new vegetable to Australia. It looks like a yellow marrow but when boiled the flesh can be forked into strands rather like spaghetti.

To cook, simply cut off a portion, scoop away the seeds and boil, unpeeled, in salted water for about 20 minutes. Then, using a fork, scoop out the flesh so that it forms strands. Toss in a little melted butter and season with freshly ground black pepper or grated nutmeg. Also delicious with fresh tomato sauce and chopped fresh basil or with any of the traditional spaghetti sauces.

EASY CAULIFLOWER MORNAY

Boil the florets of cauliflower until crispy tender. Arrange individual servings in shallow gratin dishes or scallop shells. Spread over a thin layer of thick sour cream. Cover completely with grated cheese and sprinkle with a little seasoned salt. Bake in a hot oven for about 8 minutes or until topping melts over the cauliflower forming a delicious cheese sauce.

BROCCOLI AND SNOW PEAS

500 g (1 lb) broccoli (or a
mixture of broccoli and
broccoli romanesco)
100 g (3½ oz) snow peas
1 tablespoon pine nuts
1 tablespoon oil

Separate florets of broccoli and trim snow peas, removing the little stem and any strings. Steam broccoli in a little boiling salted water until bright green and tender but still crisp. Allow approximately 3-5 minutes. Meanwhile heat oil in a wok or frying pan and fry pine nuts until a golden colour. Watch them carefully as they burn easily. Remove with a slotted spoon, then add snow peas and stir fry in the oil for a few minutes. Drain broccoli and empty straight into the peas. Toss well. Transfer to a serving dish and sprinkle with pine nuts. Serves 4-5.

BROCCOLI ROMANESCO

Although this variety of broccoli has been grown for many years in Italy it is a newcomer to Australia and is just starting to appear in specialty fruit shops during winter and early spring. It is most decorative in appearance with the tips of the spears forming a conical pattern rather like a branch of coral. The flavour is very delicate and when cooked turns a beautiful chartreuse. It is a vegetable worth growing at home.

Opposite: Broccoli and snow peas.

MUSHROOM SALAD

Use snowy white buttons, the freshest you can buy for this recipe.

250 g (½ lb) very fresh button mushrooms
1 stick celery, finely diced
½ cup fresh herbs, finely chopped (mostly parsley and chives, little mint, lemon thyme and oregano)
½ cup sunflower oil or other light salad oil
juice of 1 lemon
1 clove garlic, crushed
¼ level teaspoon ground coriander
pinch of cayenne
salt and freshly ground pepper to taste

The mushrooms should not need washing or peeling. Slice and place in a bowl with the celery and herbs. Mix oil, lemon juice and garlic together in a screw-topped jar, then add coriander and cayenne, a pinch of salt and the pepper. Shake well. Cover bowl of mushrooms with plastic and refrigerate until ready to serve. Just before serving, add dressing to mushrooms and toss lightly.

Note: Adding dressing just before serving preserves the crisp texture and the creamy pink colour of the mushrooms. Serves 4-6.

Opposite: Mushroom salad.

PERFECT ROAST POTATOES

Fuel stoves and lots of dripping around the roast possibly contribute to the success our grandmothers had with baked dinners and especially those crunchy baked potatoes, crackling crisp and puffy on the outside and soft and mealy in the middle. Here are some tips to achieve a similar result today.

The choice of potato makes a difference as some are better than others, but the most important thing is to make sure potatoes are fully mature. New potatoes are not suitable for roasting as they contain too much moisture.

Sebagos are particularly good for roasting and are usually available all year.

Russet Burbank, grown in Tasmania, is also an excellent roaster (it is the famous Idaho potato we read about in American magazines). It's a bit hard to obtain outside Tasmania and Victoria.

Kennebec, a white-skinned variety, is also good for roasting (it is used commercially for making chips) although it is not always available.

Pontiacs, the red-skinned variety, are good for roasting. They are also especially good for fluffy creamed potatoes.

Cooking: Peel the potatoes, cut into halves or quarters, parboil for 5 minutes and put around the meat during last ½ hour of cooking

A high heat is probably the most important tip of all for crunchy potatoes. Remove the roast from the oven 20 minutes before serving to rest the meat before carving. Transfer the fat and potatoes from the baking dish to a shallow cake tin, saving the precious meat sediment in the baking dish for the gravy. Return the potatoes in the cake tin to the oven which has been turned to full blast.

Another way to crisp potatoes, although it does seem like cheating, is to brown in the dripping in a frypan.

SAUTE POTATOES WITH FRESH SAGE

750 g (1½ lb) potatoes
1 medium sized white onion,
peeled and sliced
1 heaped tablespoon butter
10 large fresh sage leaves,
cut into fine strips
1 tablespoon fresh parsley,
chopped
salt and freshly ground
black pepper

Peel potatoes and cut into slices the size of a 20 cent coin.
Cover with cold water until ready to cook. Drain and pat
dry with clean teatowel.
Put butter into a large heavy frying pan. Add onion and
potato. Turn over in the butter to coat evenly. Add the
chopped sage and a good pinch of salt and cover the pan.
Cook over a low to medium heat for about 10 minutes,
shaking from time to time. Turn carefully with an egg lifter
as they brown on the bottom of the pan. Cook a further 5
minutes or so or until soft and just a little golden. Sprinkle
over the parsley and grind over black pepper. Serves 4-5.
Note: If in a hurry, parboil potato slices for 3-4 minutes
first.

DUCHESSE POTATOES

I love the way these potatoes are crispy and golden on the outside and fluffy and moist in the middle.

750 g (1½ lb) potatoes
1 egg yolk
90 g (3 oz) butter
good pinch of salt
little pepper and nutmeg

Peel and chop the potatoes. Cook in a covered pan in boiling salted water until very tender. Drain all water, then mash thoroughly. Add egg yolk and butter, reserving 1 tablespoon butter for glazing. Beat briskly with a wooden spoon, smoothing out any lumps. Season to taste with salt, pepper and nutmeg. Put the mixture into a piping bag fitted with a large meringue tube and pipe rosettes onto two greased baking trays. Brush with remaining butter. This recipe makes approximately 25. Bake in a hot oven for 15-20 minutes. Serves 8.

FRENCH POTATO SCALLOP

A great potato dish to sit beside a simple roast for casual entertaining.

1 kg (2 lb) potatoes
1 large white onion, peeled and sliced
30 g (1 oz) butter
4 eggs
300 ml (10 fl oz) cream
½ level teaspoon salt
2-3 tablespoons parmesan or romano cheese, finely grated

Peel potatoes, cut into thick slices and boil in salted water for 10 minutes. The potatoes should be tender, but still firm so that they keep their shape.
Sauté onions in butter slowly for 10 or 15 minutes to bring out all the flavour. Layer the potatoes and onions in a large shallow ovenproof dish. In a separate bowl whisk egg yolks and cream. Add salt, and fold through stiffly beaten egg whites. Pour this fluffy custard over the potatoes, then sprinkle the cheese evenly over the top. Bake for 30 minutes in a moderate oven until the top is crusty and golden and the custard is lightly set.
Serves 6-8.

ZUCCHINI WITH TOMATO

500 g (1 lb) zucchini
1 tablespoon butter
2 large ripe tomatoes, peeled
2 tablespoons water
few drops of garlic juice
(squeezed through garlic
crusher)
tiny pinch of salt
freshly ground black pepper
pinch of dried basil leaves

Slice the zucchini and fry quickly in the butter without allowing it to brown. Halve the tomatoes and squeeze out seeds. Chop the tomato flesh roughly and add to the zucchini in the pan. Add water, garlic juice, salt, pepper and basil. Cover the pan and simmer for a few minutes. The zucchini should be tender, but still a little crispy. Serves 4.

TOMATOES PROVENCALE

Very often a main course needs a 'juicy' vegetable to balance the meal. This has been an old favourite for many years now, and it's so quick and easy to prepare.

4 large ripe tomatoes
tiny pinch of salt
freshly ground black pepper
2 cups fresh white breadcrumbs
30 g (1 oz) soft butter
1 tablespoon parsley, chopped
tiny pinch of dried thyme
few drops of garlic juice

Cut each tomato in half. Place onto a buttered baking tray, cut side up. Season tomatoes with a tiny pinch of salt and a little pepper. Mix crumbs, butter, herbs and garlic juice, and place enough of the mixture on tomatoes to cover the cut surface. Bake in a hot oven for 10 minutes or until the crumbs are crispy and golden. Remove to serving plates carefully with an egg slice. Serves 8.

SCALLOPED TOMATOES

Remember this? It used to be a very popular vegetable to cook along with the 'baked dinner'.

Grease a pie plate well with butter. Put a layer of sliced tomatoes in the bottom. Sprinkle with salt, pepper and a tiny pinch of sugar. Add a little grated white onion (optional), then a layer of soft white breadcrumbs. Sprinkle with a little dried mixed herbs or dried thyme, then dot with little pieces of butter. Repeat layers until the dish is full, finishing with crumbs and butter. Bake in a moderately hot oven for 20-30 minutes.

GREEN TOMATO RELISH

One of the most delicious tomato pickles I know, this is wonderful with cold meats and grilled sausages and is especially good on cheese sandwiches.

3 kg (6 lb) green tomatoes (ripe tomatoes can be used)
500 g (1 lb) onions
1 level tablespoon salt
2 medium sized red or green capsicums
1 litre (4 cups) brown vinegar
3 cups sugar
1 level tablespoon curry powder
2 level tablespoons cornflour
4 level tablespoons Keens dry mustard (sounds a lot but quantity is correct)
1 cup additional vinegar

Chop tomatoes into large chunks, slice onion very thinly, and place the combination in a bowl. Sprinkle with salt, cover and stand overnight. Drain off liquid and put tomato and onion into a large saucepan or boiler. Add finely chopped capsicums, vinegar, sugar and curry powder. Cover pot and simmer gently for 2-2½ hours. Blend cornflour, mustard and extra vinegar together and add to the pot. Stir until the relish boils and thickens to a good consistency. Lower heat and simmmer further 20 minutes. Stir from time to time, making sure it does not catch on the bottom of the pot. Ladel into suitable sterilised jars. Seal while hot. Makes about 8 medium sized jars.

TABOULEH

A salad that's full of exciting textures and flavours, it was practically unheard of by most Australians until recent years. Tabouleh is now one of the most popular salads to serve at parties or barbecues.

½ cup burghul
½ bunch shallots
3 cups Italian parsley, chopped
¼ cup mint, chopped
2 firm ripe tomatoes
¼ cup lemon juice
¼ cup olive oil
salt and pepper to taste
1 or 2 cos lettuce hearts,
separated into cups (optional)

Soak burghul in water for ½ hour then put into a strainer. Squeeze burghul to extract as much water as possible, then transfer into a salad bowl. Trim shallots but include all the green stems and slice finely. Add parsley, mint and shallots to the burghul. Chill thoroughly. When ready to serve, halve the tomatoes and squeeze them gently to remove seeds. Chop tomato flesh into small dice, add to the salad with lemon juice and oil. Toss well together, then season to taste with salt and pepper.

Serve in a big bowl surrounded with crisp lettuce cups. Serve simply as a salad or as a finger food, spooned into the lettuce cups.

FRUIT

Glowing cherries piled up in the fruit shops just in time for Christmas are always a sign for me that summer is here at last, as is that special smell the shops seem to have during summer with the perfume of melons and stone fruit.
The abundance of fresh fruit we enjoy and use in our cooking in Australia is very much part of our special style.

Honey velvet, page 118.

HONEY VELVET

*This is a velvety honey
cream to serve with fruit*

2 level teaspoons gelatine
2 tablespoons hot water
1 plain vanilla junket tablet
1 teaspoon vanilla essence
2 cups milk
3 level tablespoons honey
1 level tablespoon brown
sugar (optional)
grated nutmeg
compote of apples or mango
coulis

Dissolve the gelatine in hot water and set aside to cool.
Crush junket tablet in a small serving bowl then stir in
vanilla essence. Put milk, honey and sugar (if used) in a
saucepan. Heat gently to blood temperature and stir to
dissolve the sugar and honey. Remove pan from the heat,
stir in the gelatine mixture and then pour it over the
crushed junket tablet. Stir quickly before sprinkling evenly
with nutmeg. Leave undisturbed until the mixture clots
(this happens almost immediately).
Place in the refrigerator and chill until the gelatine sets.
The result is a surprisingly smooth and velvety cream
almost like a bavarois. Serve with a compote of apples or a
mango coulis. Serves 4.
Note: Honey velvet is very quick and easy to make but it
can be tricky. The same rules apply as for making junket —
the milk temperature must be just right.

APPLE COMPOTE

500 g (1 lb) Granny Smith
apples
2-3 level tablespoons sugar
¾ cup water (or ½ cup
water and ¼ cup white
wine)
strip of thinly peeled
orange rind
2 cloves

Peel, quarter and core the apples then cut them into thick slices. Place them with the remaining ingredients in a saucepan and simmer for 10-15 minutes (less if apples are new season). To retain shape of apples it is advisable to cook them uncovered or with the saucepan lid loosely fitted. Pour into a bowl and chill. Remove cloves and orange peel before serving.

MANGO COULIS

Purée the flesh of one large ripe mango in a food processor. Thin with fresh orange juice if desired.

HOT PASSIONFRUIT SOUFFLE

This is a simple straight forward method which is delicious and very successful, although as with most souffles it does collapse quickly after baking. An additional step in the recipe means extra last minute preparation but it does produce a souffle that will hold for five minutes or more after baking.

4 tablespoons strained fresh passionfruit pulp (about 6 large passionfruit)
4 egg whites
½ cup castor sugar
¼ cup water
6 small souffle dishes

A simple way to obtain the juice from the passionfruit is to place the pulp in a food processor and process for a few seconds, then strain. This helps to release the seeds from the flesh (the blades won't chop through the seeds if processed quickly). Have the egg whites ready in the bowl of the electric mixer. Place sugar and water in a saucepan and stir to dissolve then brush down sides and boil until thick enough to form a soft toffee (to test dip a teaspoon of syrup into a cup cold water). While the syrup cooks, whip the egg whites until stiff. Pour syrup straight onto whites, then add the passionfruit juice and continue beating for a minute. Fill the buttered souffle dishes level with top. Bake in a moderate oven for 12-15 minutes. Serve immediately sprinkled with sifted icing sugar. Have softly whipped cream (could be flavoured with Kirsch) on the table. Serves 4 to 6.

Method 2: After testing the syrup in cold water, add the passionfruit juice. Continue cooking this syrup, shaking over the heat until it returns to the toffee stage, then beat into the stiffly beaten egg whites.

ICED PASSIONFRUIT SOUFFLE

6 eggs, separated
⅔ cup castor sugar
2 tablespoons lemon juice
1 teaspoon finely grated
lemon rind
½ cup hot water
1 level tablespoon gelatine
½ cup fresh passionfruit
pulp
300 mls (10 fl oz)
cream

Place the egg whites into a large mixing bowl, and the yolks into a small heatproof bowl (or top half of a double boiler). Add ⅓ cup sugar, the lemon juice and rind to the yolks and whisk over simmering water until frothy, being careful not to scramble the mixture by overcooking. Pour hot water into a cup. Sprinkle in the gelatine and at the same time whisk briskly with a fork to dissolve. Add to the yolks and remove from the heat. Cool and add passionfruit pulp. Whip egg whites until stiff, gradually beating in the remaining ⅓ cup sugar. Whip the cream softly then fold the egg whites and cream through the passionfruit mixture. Pour into a glass serving dish. Serves 6-8.

LEMON SOUFFLE

Use the same recipe as the passionfruit souffle omitting the passionfruit pulp but increasing the lemon juice to ½ cup and the lemon rind to 2 level teaspoons.

PASSIONFRUIT FLUMMERY

1 sachet (3 level teaspoons)
gelatine
½ cup sugar
2 level tablespoons plain
flour
1 cup water
1 cup fresh orange juice
⅓ cup fresh passionfruit
pulp (about 4 passionfruit)

Put gelatine, sugar and flour into a saucepan then add some of the measured water and blend with the back of a spoon to smooth out any lumps. Gradually add the remaining water and stir until the mixture boils. Reduce the heat and simmer for a minute or two then pour into a large mixing bowl and allow to cool. Add the orange juice and passionfruit pulp. Refrigerate until the mixture starts to set around edges of bowl. Whip with electric mixer until thick (usually takes 5-10 minutes). Pour into a pretty glass bowl and refrigerate until set. Serve with pouring cream. Serves 4-5.

Note: Use a Mixmaster or Kenwood to whip flummery. A food processor is not suitable for this recipe.

ITALIAN STYLE PEACHES

6 large slipstone peaches
125 g (4 oz) coconut or
almond macaroons (crushed)
2 egg yolks
1 level tablespoon sugar
1 tablespoon soft butter

Cut peaches in halves leaving the skins on but discarding the stones. Using a dessertspoon scoop a little flesh from the centre of each peach. Mix this peach mixture with the crushed macaroons, egg yolks, sugar and butter. Mix well together then pile back into peaches to form a little mound. Bake in a buttered baking dish for approximately ¾ hour. Serve immediately with whipped cream. Serves about 8.

AEROPLANE JELLY WHIP

A recipe that was very popular in Australia during the 1940s this is surprisingly good and very easy to make.

1 can (375 ml) unsweetened
evaporated milk, chilled
1 packet lemon jelly
1 cup boiling water
3 or 4 fresh passionfruit

Empty jelly crystals into a small bowl, add boiling water and stir until dissolved. Chill until jelly is at the wobbly, half-set stage. In a separate bowl, whip evaporated milk until thick, then beat in the half-set jelly and the passionfruit pulp. Pour quickly into a serving bowl. Refrigerate until set. Serves 6-8.

MULBERRY CRUMBLE

Mulberry trees feature in many suburban gardens, usually grown in the first place to satisfy the armies of fat silkworms (residing in shoe boxes) with insatiable appetites and needing a constant supply of mulberry leaves. Early in the summer the trees are laden with fat juicy berries. Here is a delicious way to use them.

1 apple, peeled and cored
1 cup water
3 cups ripe mulberries
1 tablespoon sugar

CRUMBLE:
100 g (3½ oz) butter
½ cup brown sugar (firmly packed)
½ cup SR flour
½ cup rolled oats or desiccated coconut

Slice the apple and cook in the water in a small saucepan about 15 minutes. Add the mulberries and sugar and simmer for a further five minutes. Pour into a shallow ovenproof dish or pie plate.

Rub the butter into the flour, add the brown sugar and oats then mix evenly. Place mixture over the mulberries in small even heaps. Bake in a moderate oven for 30 minutes. Serve warm with cream or ice cream. Serves 5.

Note: Remove mulberry stains on fingers by rubbing with unripe red mulberries.

APPLE CRUMBLE

Cook 6 peeled and sliced Granny Smith apples in ¾ cup water with 1 tablespoon of sugar until soft and fluffy. Pour into a pie plate cover with crumble topping and cook as above.

KING SALAD

This exciting tropical salad was the invention of television cook, Bernard King. Bernard grew up in Queensland, so adding passionfruit to a French dressing to serve over tropical fruit seemed perfectly natural. It's a wonderful looking salad and the flavours team beautifully.

2 firm ripe avocados
1 small (or ½ large) firm ripe papaw
3×250 g (½ lb) size smoked Snowy Mountain trout, skinned and filleted
1 or 2 small white (mildly flavoured) onions, peeled and thinly sliced

PASSIONFRUIT DRESSING

2 tablespoons light salad oil
2 tablespoons lemon juice
juice of 1 small orange
2 large passionfruit

Halve the avocados, peel carefully and cut flesh into thickish slivers. Peel the papaw, cut into thick slices, scooping away the pips. Arrange the avocado and the papaw in alternate slices on one half of a large flat platter. Arrange the smoked trout fillets on the other side. Cut an onion into paper thin slices and scatter over the salad. Make a passionfruit dressing by combining oil, juices and passionfruit pulp in a screw-topped jar. Shake well then pour over the fruit. Serve icy cold as a first course. Serves 6-8.

APPLE SNOW

1 kg (2 lb) fresh new season
Granny Smith apples
(usually about six)
2 cloves
½ cup water
2 egg whites
¼ cup sugar

Peel, quarter and core the apples then place them into a
saucepan with the cloves and water. Cover and simmer
gently until the apples are fluffy then tip them into a
colander to drain and cool (for successful Apple Snow, the
apples should be fairly dry). Remove cloves.
Whip the egg whites until stiff and white then gradually
whip in the sugar. Add the apples then beat with rotary
beater or Mixmaster until they are white and frothy. Pile
into a pretty serving dish and serve with homemade boiled
custard (the recipe is on page 157) made using the egg
yolks. Serves 6.

Opposite: Apple snow.

STRAWBERRIES VICTORIA

*Oliver Shaul developed
this recipe at the 1956
Olympics in Victoria.*

2 punnets of strawberries
⅓ cup sugar
**2 tablespoons Curacao or
Cointreau**
2 passionfruit

Wash and hull the strawberries then place in a bowl and
add the sugar, liqueur and passionfruit pulp. Stir gently
and cover. Refrigerate for several hours allowing the
flavours to mingle and mellow. Spoon into serving dishes
and serve with whipped cream. Serves 6.

STRAWBERRY SORBET

**600 g (20 oz) frozen,
unsweetened strawberries**
¾ cup sugar
1 orange, freshly squeezed
½ cup thickened cream

Partially thaw strawberries then transfer into a food
processor with the sugar and orange juice. Process until
smooth. Pour into an ice cream tray or aluminium cake tin.
Refreeze until icy. Break up, and smooth out in food
processor. Pour in the cream and continue beating few
seconds more. Return to the container and cover with
plastic. Refreeze until ready to serve.

*Opposite: Strawberries
Victoria.*

STRAWBERRY PARFAIT

A recipe for strawberries in a luscious vanilla cream that is easy to make and not too rich. It is best served in individual glasses.

1 punnet strawberries
4 level tablespoons sugar
2½ level teaspoons gelatine
¼ cup cold water
1 cup milk
1 teaspoon vanilla essence
½ cup cream, chilled
pink colouring

Wash and hull the strawberries. Slice into a small bowl, sprinkle with sugar and leave for ½ hour or until they become juicy. Mix the gelatine and water in a small bowl and stand in a pan of simmering water until the gelatine is clear. Stir into the strawberries, mix well, then add the milk and vanilla. Whip the cream, fold through the mixture, adding a few drops of pink colouring to improve colour. Place in the refrigerator until the mixture starts to thicken. Stir to distribute berries, then spoon into parfait glasses or tall-stemmed wine glasses. Refrigerate until set. Serves 4-5.

STRAWBERRIES IN TOFFEE

You can make a spectacular entrance with a plate of these gorgeous strawberries—they look as if they've been wrapped in cellophane! It's very quick and easy to do once you have mastered the art of making a simple toffee.

1 punnet large strawberries
1 cup sugar
½ cup water
pinch of cream of tartar

Grease a flat baking tray with butter and place near the stove in readiness. Wash the strawberries and drain well (they need to be dry before using). Do not remove hulls or stems (if the stems are short, you will need a pair of tweezers to save burning fingers). Place sugar, water and cream of tartar into a saucepan and stir over a low heat until all the sugar crystals have dissolved. Brush away any stray sugar crystals from the sides of the pan with a wet pastry brush. Boil without stirring until the toffee just starts to show the first signs of pale gold at the edges of the pan.

Remove from heat and tilt the pan to one side. Hold strawberries by stems and dip straight down into toffee and then straight onto the buttered tray. The toffee will set in a few minutes. Serve immediately as a bon bon with after dinner coffee. Serves approximately 8.

Note: There are other fruits suitable to glaze with toffee, including seedless sultana grapes separated into little bunches, big sweet black cherries or mandarin segments. Orange segments are particularly delicious although a little tricky to do as the juice tends to water down the toffee. Use a fork to dip the mandarin and orange segments. Set on a greased tray and serve in little paper cups.

RHUBARB AND STRAWBERRY COMPOTE

Old fashioned rhubarb is making a comeback in Australia. This recipe for a combination of rhubarb and strawberries looks very pretty when served in an antique glass bowl to serve at the table. The rhubarb seems to make the colour of the strawberries appear a most beautiful bright red.

1 bunch rhubarb (about 20 sticks or 4 cups chopped)
3 to 4 heaped tablespoons sugar
½ cup water
1 teaspoon finely grated orange rind
1 or 2 punnets strawberries (hulled)

Chop the rhubarb into finger lengths and put it into a saucepan with the sugar and water. Cover and simmer gently for 5-7 minutes (try not to let it overcook and go stringy). Pour into a serving dish and add the orange rind. Cool slightly, then stir through the hulled strawberries. Chill thoroughly and serve with softly whipped thickened cream. Serves 6-8.

Note: When mulberries are in season they are also delicious lightly stewed and added to the strawberry/rhubarb combination.

PEACH MELBA

Dame Nelly Melba had a private tasting of the very first 'Peach Melba' in the world. She was lunching alone in her room at the Savoy Hotel in London, when towards the end of the meal a little silver dish arrived and was uncovered before her to reveal a most delicious looking dessert. On the tray was a little note informing her that Mr Escoffier had prepared the dessert in honour of her visit. Dame Nelly loved the combination of peaches and fresh raspberries and enquired if it had a name. The answer came back that Mr Escoffier would be honoured if he might name it 'Pêche Melba'.

4 ripe slipstone peaches
½ cup sugar
2 cups water
1 vanilla bean or ½ teaspoon pure vanilla essence
1 cup fresh raspberries
2 level tablespoons sugar
2-3 teaspoons lemon juice
4 scoops vanilla ice cream

Peel the peaches, cut into halves and discard the stones. Poach peaches in a saucepan with sugar, water, vanilla bean or essence – do not overcook. Transfer the peaches and syrup into a dish to cool, keeping the peaches covered with the syrup to prevent discolouration. Cover the dish with plastic wrap and refrigerate until icy cold. For the raspberry sauce, puree raspberries with sugar and lemon juice in food processor. When serving, place a scoop of vanilla ice cream into each serving dish, add the peaches and spoon over the raspberry sauce. Serves 4.

APRICOT AND ALMOND JAM

Australian dried apricots are considered by many to be the best in the world and dried apricot jam must be the easiest jam in the world to make. It is especially delicious served with warm croissants.

500 g (1 lb) dried apricots
1¾ litre (7 cups) water
1.5 kg (3 lb) sugar
½ cup blanched almond halves
½ teaspoon almond essence

Soak the apricots in the water overnight. Next day put the apricots plus any liquid into a large saucepan or boiler. Simmer covered for approximately ½ hour or until it becomes soft and pulpy. Add the sugar and stir until dissolved. Boil rapidly until setting stage, stirring occasionally as it is inclined to stick on the bottom. Stir in the almonds and essence, then bottle and seal while still hot. Makes about 5 jars.

PLUM JAM

Homemade plum jam has a memorable flavour rather like a luscious port.

2 kg (4 lb) red plums
1 cup water (less if plums are juicy)
juice of ½ lemon
1.5 kg (3 lb) sugar

Wash the plums and drain well, then cut in halves and remove stones. Leave the skins on for the tangy plum flavour. Place plums, water and lemon juice into a large saucepan or boiler then cover and simmer over a low heat until well cooked, approximately ¾ hour. Add sugar and stir until dissolved. Boil rapidly uncovered until jam reaches setting point, usually after ½ hour, but it is advisable to start testing after 15 minutes. The jam is ready when it starts to run off the spoon in a chunky flake, but confirm with the cold saucer test. Bottle and seal while hot. Makes about 5 medium sized jars.

Note: Rather like a good red wine, plum jam actually improves with age. Allow to mature for a few weeks before using.

BRANDIED GRAPES

500 g (1 lb) green sultana
grapes (seedless)
2 tablespoons fresh
orange juice
2 tablespoons honey
2 tablespoons brandy

Wash the grapes and pull away from stems. Pour orange juice, warmed honey and brandy into a bowl and mix to combine, then add the grapes. Toss well in the mixture, cover, and refrigerate until icy cold. Serve the grapes in tall stemmed glasses topped with a little softly whipped thickened cream or with sour cream whipped with brown sugar. Serves 4.

FRESH APRICOT AND MUSTARD SEED CHUTNEY

Fresh apricots spiked with mustard seeds are a delicious combination. This recipe makes 10 medium sized jars.

2 kg (4 lb) fresh apricots
500 g (1 lb) plums
500 g (1 lb) onions, peeled and chopped
500 g (1 lb) brown or white sugar
500 g (1 lb) sultanas
3 cups (750 ml bottle) brown or white vinegar
2 level tablespoons mustard seeds
1 level tablespoon salt
2 level teaspoons each tumeric, cinnamon and coriander
1 tablespoon mild sweet chilli sauce (if using a hot chilli sauce reduce quantity to taste)
grated rind and juice 2 oranges
grated rind and juice of 2 lemons
4 cloves garlic, crushed
2 teaspoons green ginger, grated

Halve the apricots and plums, discard the stones, then put fruit into a large boiler with the remaining ingredients. Bring the contents to the boil then reduce the heat. Simmer very slowly for about 2 hours or until you have a good chutney consistency. Watch carefully during the last hour of cooking to make sure the chutney doesn't catch to the bottom of the pan. Bottle and seal while hot.

HOT PEACH AND PLUM CHUTNEY

This recipe contains chunky pieces of peach in a spicy plum sauce spiked with chilli and green ginger.

1 kg (2 lb) slipstone peaches
1 kg (2 lb) blood plums
1 large onion, peeled and chopped
2 cups white vinegar
2 cups sugar
½ cup raisins
¼ cup green ginger, peeled and finely chopped
2 level tablespoons black mustard seeds
1 level tablespoon garam masala
1 level tablespoon salt
6 cloves garlic, crushed
½ cup dates, chopped
4 chillies (if using the very hot birds-eye chillies, reduce to 2)

Peel the peaches and chop into chunks, then halve the unpeeled plums and discard the stones from both fruits. Put the fruit into a large saucepan or boiler with all ingredients except chilli. To prepare chillies: cut into halves lengthways, run under cold running water to remove seeds, then cut into strips and add to the pot. Do take care to wash hands thoroughly after handling chillies and avoid touching eyes while preparing. Bring the mixture to the boil, then lower the heat and simmer for 1 hour, stirring occasionally to prevent fruit catching on the bottom. Ladle into heated jars and seal with a non-metal covering. Makes 4-5 medium jars.

Note: 1 tablespoon chilli oil (available in Chinese grocery stores) could be used instead of fresh chillies.

PUDDINGS

Everyone has some very special memories of the puddings they loved as a child. Mention bread and butter custard with plump sultanas or sago plum pudding to most Australians and it starts a flood of memories, as does the thought of Grandma's featherlight dumplings and creamy rice pudding encrusted with delicious golden skin.

So if you're longing for a taste of nostalgia and you have lost Mum's old recipes, you may find your favourite here. Marshallow pavlova smothered with cream and fresh fruit is still just about the most popular party dessert in Australia. The recipe in this chapter is a beauty and not quite as sweet as some.

Marshmallow pavlova, page 140.

MARSHMALLOW PAVLOVA—BASIC RECIPE

This is a good recipe (not quite as sweet as some) with some hints for success.

4 egg whites (should be as fresh as possible)
good pinch of salt
1 heaped cup castor sugar
1 teaspoon white vinegar
1 level tablespoon cornflour (wheaten cornflour for preference)
½ teaspoon vanilla essence
300 ml (10 fl.oz) thickened cream, whipped
4 bananas
3 passionfruit
1 punnet strawberries

Preheat oven to hot. Cover a greased flat baking tray with gladbake or a split open oven bag. Grease well with butter, sprinkle with cornflour and tap off excess (the cornflour gives a nice dry surface under the pavlova).
Using a 18 cm (7 inch) cake tin as a guide, mark out a circle on the tray with a skewer.
Beat egg whites and salt until stiff. Add sugar 1 heaped tablespoon at a time until all sugar has been added. When finished, the meringue should be thick and shiny. Stir in vinegar, cornflour and vanilla, stir gently then pile onto prepared tray. The mixture should stay roughly in the marked circle, simply smooth over the top (it is important not to make the mistake of scooping out the centre). The mixture should be about 6 cm (2½ inches) high for a good marshmallow centre. Drop oven temperature to very slow before placing the pavlova in the oven. Bake for 1¼ hours. Remove from oven and cool for a few minutes then turn upside down onto a flat serving plate. Remove paper or ovenwrap carefully. The centre will sink slightly as the

pavlova cools. When cold, fill with whipped cream and top with sliced bananas, passionfruit pulp and whole strawberries. Serves 8-10.

TURNING THE PAVLOVA UPSIDE DOWN

If you don't like this idea (it's really quite easy when you get the knack), simply bake the pavlova directly on a greased plate (see following).

PAVLOVA BAKED ON THE PLATE

This method uses six eggs and the meringue is baked directly on the serving dish.

6 egg whites
good pinch of salt
1½ cups castor sugar
1½ teaspoons white vinegar
1½ level tablespoons cornflour
1 teaspoon vanilla essence
2 cups thickened cream, whipped
5 or 6 bananas or 2 punnets strawberries
4 passionfruit

Make up the meringue as in basic marshmallow pavlova recipe. Grease pavlova plate with butter, dust with cornflour, tap away excess. Make meringue as in basic recipe and pile into the centre of the plate. Make sure the height is at least 6 cm (2½ inches) high. Use a spatula to rough the surface. Try to shape the sides so that they slope in towards the centre. Bake as before, allowing about 1½-1¾ hours cooking time. Fill with whipped cream and sliced fruit when cold and preferably no more than 1 hour before serving. Serves about 12.

PAVLOVA FOR A CROWD

This is a recipe that I make often when entertaining a crowd. It is shaped into an oval and turned out either onto a tray or onto a large meat platter.

9 egg whites
good pinch of salt
500 g (1 lb) castor sugar
2 teaspoons white vinegar
1 teaspoon vanilla essence
2 level tablespoons cornflour
600-750 ml (1-1¼ pints) thickened cream, whipped
6 bananas
6-8 passionfruit
2 punnets strawberries (small tumble packs are good for pavlova)

The method is the same as for the basic recipe for marshmallow pavlova. Shape the meringue into an oval, about 18 cm (7 inches) by 23 cm (9 inches) and 6 cm (2½ inches) high. It usually fits diagonally across a normal sized baking tray. Flatten the top of the meringue with a spatula. Preheat oven (see page 140), turn to very slow. Bake for about 2 hours. Stand for a few minutes. Turn out onto the serving tray (the easiest way is to put the tray over the pavlova gently, then carefully turn so the tray is underneath). Remove the paper and cool. The centre will sink gradually as the pavlova cools. It's not a bad idea to mark a small oval in the centre with the point of a vegetable knife so that the centre sinks evenly, leaving the outside edge intact. Fill with cream and fruit when quite cold. Serves 18-20.
Note: It's best to fill no sooner than 1 hour before serving.

APPLE ROLY

Mention this pudding to people of my generation and they usually say the best part was the toffee on the sides of the dish!

1 cup SR flour
50 g (1½ oz) butter
3 tablespoons water
raspberry jam
2 large Granny Smith apples
1 cup hot water
½ cup sugar
1 heaped tablespoons soft butter

Sift flour into a small basin. Rub in butter and make into a dough by adding water. Knead lightly, and roll out thinly on a floured surface into a rectangular shape. Spread with an even layer of raspberry jam. Grate apple coarsely over the dough and cover evenly. Roll up like a Swiss roll and put into a well buttered casserole dish, shaping roll around to fit the dish.

Make a syrup by boiling water, sugar and butter for a couple of minutes. Pour over the roll. Cut several slits in the top of the roll and brush with a little milk. Bake uncovered in a hot oven for approximately ¾ hour. Serve hot with homemade boiled custard (the recipe is on page 157). Serves 6.

PANCAKES

Thick pancakes or flapjacks are a great favourite with teenagers. This is a foolproof recipe.

2 cups SR flour (white or wholemeal)
½ level teaspoon salt
⅓ cup castor sugar
2 eggs
2 tablespoons melted butter
1 teaspoon vanilla essence
1½ cups milk
butter for cooking

IDEAS FOR TOPPING

butter and honey or maple syrup
jam and whipped cream
sugar and fresh lemons
spicy cooked apple
fresh berries and cream

Sift flour and salt into a bowl. Mix in sugar and make a well in the middle. Add unbeaten eggs, melted butter, vanilla, and half the milk. Beat well to remove lumps, then blend in the remaining milk. Heat a frypan and grease well with a small knob of butter. Allow 2 tablespoons batter for each pancake. Pour the batter into greased frypan and cook until surface is covered with bubbles, then turn over and lightly cook the other side. Stack pancakes on a plate over boiling water. Serve hot with selected toppings. Makes approximately 16.

LEMON PANCAKES

This is an 'almost' no fail recipe for tender thin pancakes. The SR flour, a traditionally Australian ingredient, makes them light and tender. These pancakes are simply delicious eaten hot from the pan with sugar and fresh lemon juice

1½ cups SR flour
½ level teaspoon salt
¼ cup castor sugar
2 eggs
2 tablespoons melted butter
1¾ cups milk
few drops of vanilla essence
3 or 4 lemons
butter for cooking
sugar for cooked pancakes

Sift flour and salt into a bowl. Add sugar. Make a well in the centre and break in eggs. Add melted butter and half the milk. Beat well to smooth out any lumps, then gradually add remaining milk and vanilla.

Put a large saucepan half filled with water on to boil (this is to keep pancakes hot after cooking). Heat a little knob of butter in a frying pan, allow to turn nut brown, then pour off and wipe out with kitchen paper (this seasons the pan). Allow approximately 2-3 tablespoons batter for an average sized frying pan (less for crepe pans). Heat a little dot of butter in pan and, when sizzling hot, pour in batter, twisting pan quickly to cover the base (pour away any excess). Cook over high heat, turning once.

Place a plate over the steaming water and as the pancakes cook stack on the plate, sprinkling with sugar and lemon juice as you go. When all are cooked, roll up and serve hot. Serves 4-5.

BREAD AND BUTTER CUSTARD

The old puddings that our grannies used to make always have an appeal (especially with men). Once they were reserved only for family occasions, but these days they are often served at dinner parties as a special treat. This is especially delicious if served just warm with lightly sugared fresh raspberries and softly whipped cream.

4 eggs
½ cup sugar
600 mls (2½ cups) milk
1 teaspoon vanilla essence
1 tablespoon sultanas
2 or 3 slices buttered bread
with the crusts removed

Break eggs into a mixing bowl, add sugar, vanilla and milk. Whisk with an egg beater to combine thoroughly. Pour into a lightly buttered ovenproof dish. Add sultanas. Cut bread into fingers or triangles and float on top of custard, buttered side up.

Bake 'au bain-marie' (standing in a baking dish of cold water) in a moderately slow oven for approximately 1½-2 hours. The custard is cooked when it is set and the topping is golden brown and slightly crispy at the edges. Serve warm or cold as a single sweet or with softly whipped cream and fresh or stewed fruit. Serves 4 to 5.

LEMON DELICIOUS PUDDING

Everyone seems to like this pudding.

½ cup SR flour
1 cup sugar
grated rind of 1 large lemon
4 tablespoons lemon juice
4 level tablespoons melted butter
3 eggs, separated
1½ cups milk

Put flour, sugar and lemon rind into a basin. Add lemon juice, melted butter and egg yolks. Beat until thoroughly mixed, then stir in milk gradually. Beat egg whites in a separate bowl until stiff and white, then gradually pour in the batter. Pour into a well buttered ovenproof dish. Stand the dish in a baking dish of cold water and bake in a moderate oven for approximately 1 hour. Serve warm with vanilla ice cream. Serves 6.

FEATHER DATE PUDDING

This old Australian country recipe is a classic pudding and well worth reviving.

1 cup firmly packed dates
1 cup milk
¼ cup sugar
2 level tablespoons butter
1 scant level teaspoon bicarbonate of soda
1 cup SR flour

Place chopped dates, milk, sugar and butter into a saucepan. Heat gently until almost boiling, then add well crushed bicarbonate of soda, stir gently then remove from heat and cool. Stir in the flour and mix well. Put the mixture into a small well buttered pudding basin and cover with two sheets greased foil or gladbake. Tie with string, or cover with a clip lid. Lower basin into a large saucepan of boiling water which should come half way up the sides of the basin. Cover saucepan with a lid and simmer pudding gently for 1½ hours. Replace with boiling water as necessary but try not to let the water go off the simmer. Turn out, and serve hot with boiled custard (the recipe is on page 157). Serves 6.

GOLDEN SYRUP PUDDING

Remember this pudding, and the way the golden syrup formed a wonderful spongy top when turned out of the basin?

3 level tablespoons golden syrup
125 g (4 oz) butter
½ cup castor sugar
1 teaspoon vanilla essence
2 eggs
1½ cups SR flour
½ cup milk

Grease a small pudding basin well with butter. Pour golden syrup in the bottom. Cream butter, sugar and vanilla essence. Beat in the eggs one at a time, fold in sifted flour, then stir in milk. Add the pudding mixture to the basin on top of the golden syrup. Cover top of basin with two sheets of foil or gladbake, greasing the layer next to the pudding so it does not stick. Tie well with string and lower into a pot of *boiling* water. The water should come halfway up the sides of the basin. Cover the pot and simmer gently for 1½ hours. Remove basin and stand for a few minutes before turning out. Serve with homemade boiled custard (the recipe is on page 157). Serves 6.

Opposite: Golden syrup pudding.

MACADAMIA ICE CREAM

Pure natural flavours make this a delicious ice cream. The Regent Hotel in Sydney makes a wonderful macadamia nut ice cream; this is a loose translation of that recipe.

6 egg yolks
600 ml (20 fl oz) thickened cream
1½ cups milk
1 scant cup raw sugar
1 level tablespoon honey
2 teaspoons vanilla essence
60 g (2 oz) macadamia nuts, candied (see below) or substitute Vienna almonds

Place egg yolks, cream, milk, raw sugar and honey into a saucepan. Stir over very low heat until custard thickens slightly, making sure it does not boil. The custard is ready when it will hold the trace of your finger on the back of the spoon. Strain mixture into suitable container such as a shallow aluminium loaf tin. Cool quickly by standing dish in cold water. Freeze, then break up and beat with an electric mixer until double in volume. Add vanilla and finely chopped nuts. Return quickly to freezing tray, cover with plastic and freeze.

CANDIED MACADAMIA NUTS

Place 2 level tablespoons sugar into a heavy frying pan and shake over medium heat until golden and clear. Add macadamia nuts, stir quickly to coat, then scrape out onto a greased baking tray to set. Chop finely before adding to ice cream.

Opposite: Macadamia ice cream.

PASSIONFRUIT ICE CREAM

This is a good choice to serve when entertaining overseas guests, especially during summer when raspberries and mangoes are in season.

6 egg yolks
¾ cup sugar
½ cup water
1½ cups thickened cream, lightly whipped
½ cup sieved passionfruit pulp (8-10 large passionfruit)
2 tablespoons Grand Marnier

Place egg yolks into a food processor or the small bowl of an electric mixer. Put sugar and water into a saucepan and stir over medium heat to dissolve sugar. Brush down sides of the pan to free of sugar crystals with a wet pastry brush. Boil the syrup until it reaches the soft ball stage (when a little syrup forms a soft ball in cold water). With the food processor or mixer going at top speed, pour in the syrup in a steady stream. Cool for ½ hour, then fold through whipped cream, passionfruit juice and Grand Marnier.

Pour into 8-10 small souffle dishes or tiny moulds (small oval moulds look pretty). Freeze until firm, then cover with foil. Unmould onto flat serving plates and surround with fresh summer fruit (a few slices of mango or nectarine and fresh raspberries or strawberries). Serves 8-10, depending on size of moulds.

GRAND MARNIER ICE CREAM

Make up passionfruit ice cream recipe omitting the strained passionfruit. Increase the Grand Marnier to 3 tablespoons. Do not be tempted to add more Grand Marnier or the ice cream will not freeze.

GOLDEN SYRUP DUMPLINGS

SYRUP
1⅓ cups water
¾ cup lightly packed brown
sugar (or ½ cup white
sugar)
2 level tablespoons golden
syrup
tiny squeeze of lemon juice
1 slightly rounded
tablespoon butter

DUMPLINGS
1 cup SR flour
1 slightly rounded
tablespoon butter
1 egg
1-2 tablespoons milk

Make the syrup first. Put water, sugar, syrup, butter and tiny squeeze of lemon juice into a wide, shallow saucepan. Stir occasionally to dissolve sugar and bring to the boil. Meanwhile, sift flour into a mixing bowl. Rub in butter, make a well (hole) and add egg and milk. Mix gently just to combine ingredients (don't overmix). Form into little balls with floured hands or alternatively drop from spoon into the boiling syrup. Cover immediately with a lid (the steam is necessary for fluffy dumplings). Lower heat and simmer until dumplings are cooked and well risen, about 10-15 minutes, depending on size. Don't overcook or they will be tough. Serve immediately with cream or boiled custard (the recipe is on page 157.) Serves 4.

SAGO PLUM PUDDING

4 level tablespoons sago
1 cup milk
1 level teaspoon
bicarbonate of soda
¾ cup lightly packed brown
sugar
1½ cups lightly packed soft
breadcrumbs (white or
wholegrain bread)
1 cup sultanas
½ cup dates, chopped
pinch of salt
2 small eggs
3 level tablespoons melted
butter
6 cup pudding basin, well
greased

Put sago into a basin, pour over the milk and soak overnight in the refrigerator. Next day, empty sago and milk into a mixing bowl. Add the soda and stir in the remaining ingredients. Mix well. Put a circle of buttered greaseproof in the bottom of the basin. Pack in the pudding. Cover with buttered paper, then cover tightly with a clip-on lid or with two sheets of foil tied with string. Lower into a boiler of boiling water (to come half up sides). Cover pan and simmer for 3 hours. Serve hot with boiled custard (page 157) or vanilla custard sauce. Serves 6.

VANILLA CUSTARD SAUCE

Serve as a chilled sauce on a big dinner plate under a perfectly poached pear. Try also as a cold sauce with fresh fruit or as a contrast of textures and flavours with hot puddings and pastries.

4 egg yolks
¼ cup sugar (could also be raw sugar)
1¾ cups milk
¼ cup cream
thin strip of lemon rind
1 teaspoon vanilla essence

Beat egg yolks with sugar in a bowl. Heat milk and cream slowly with lemon peel, and when almost boiling whisk into bowl containing yolks and sugar. Return mixture to the saucepan and cook over *very low heat*, stirring all the time with a wooden spoon (a figure eight movement when stirring ensures even cooking). The custard is ready when it leaves the trace of your finger on the back of the spoon. Remove from heat, remove peel and stir in vanilla. Pour into a bowl and cover. Chill before serving.

CREAMED RICE

Creamed rice is an old fashioned recipe that Grandmothers always seemed to make on Sundays when cooking the baked dinner. There is a special tip while cooking the rice to make it extra creamy. You will discover this when reading the recipe.

4 level tablespoons Calrose short grain rice
¼ cup sugar
3½ cups milk
2 tablespoons cream (optional)

Place rice, sugar and milk into an ovenproof dish. Bake in a slow oven (or coolest part of oven if cooking with a baked dinner). While rice is cooking stir from time to time as this makes the rice very creamy. The rice is ready when the milk is the consistency of thickened cream, usually 2-2½ hours. Stir in the cream. Serve warm with fluffy stewed apples. Serves 5.

SHERRY TRIFLE

When I was growing up weddings and 21st birthdays were usually held in the local hall and trifle was always served. Even though it wasn't always the best trifle in the world, it always seemed to taste good to me. Maybe it's time it made a comeback!

2 red jellies (Aeroplane Tasmanian Raspberry)
1 litre (4 cups) milk
4 level tablespoons custard powder
4 level tablespoons sugar
2 teaspoons vanilla essence
1 cup cream, whipped
1 sponge cake
3 tablespoons good sweet sherry
1 small can sliced peaches, drained
3 cooking apples, peeled and sliced with a little sugar and water
or 1 can dessert apple slices
additional whipped cream
nutmeg
chopped nuts

Make the jellies according to the instructions on the packet and pour into a square cake tin. Chill until set, then cut into cubes.

Put custard powder into a saucepan, stir in a small quantity of milk and blend together with a spoon. Stir in remaining milk, sugar and vanilla. Stir over a medium heat until thick. Pour into a bowl and when cool, fold in cream. Break sponge cake into pieces and place a layer in the bottom of a serving dish. Sprinkle with sherry, add alternate layers of fruit and custard, then repeat, finishing with layer of custard. Top with the cubes of jelly, then decorate with whipped cream and sprinkle with chopped nuts and grated nutmeg. Serves 8-10.

BOILED CUSTARD

A good basic recipe for a hot pouring custard over steamed or baked puddings.

2 cups milk
2 to 3 level tablespoons sugar
thin strip of lemon peel (optional)
2 level tablespoons custard powder
extra ¼ cup milk
2 egg yolks
1 teaspoon vanilla essence

Put milk and sugar into a saucepan with lemon peel. Bring to the boil. Meanwhile, mix custard powder and extra milk together in a small basin to smooth out any lumps. Add to the milk and stir constantly until the custard boils and thickens. Mix egg yolks and vanilla in basin. Tip a little hot custard onto yolks, whisk quickly then pour back into the saucepan. Return to a *very low* heat and stir for minute or so without boiling to cook yolks (heat of custard is usually sufficient). Remove peel and serve hot with steamed puddings, etc.

If serving cold, pour into a basin and cover tightly with plastic (put right down onto surface to prevent a skin forming) and refrigerate. When chilled this custard thickens to the consistency of softly whipped cream. Thin with a little pouring cream if necessary.

BANANA CUSTARD

Make up basic recipe for custard. Slice one large or two medium bananas into a basin, pour over hot custard, making sure the bananas are completely covered. Cover and chill before serving. Best served within a few hours as bananas have a short life in the refrigerator.

CHOCOLATE SAUCE PUDDING

1 cup SR flour
1 level tablespoon cocoa
½ cup castor sugar
1 egg
2 teaspoons vanilla essence
½ cup milk
60 g (2 oz) butter, melted

TOPPING
1 level tablespoon cocoa
1 cup lightly packed brown
sugar
¼ teaspoon instant coffee
powder
1¾ cups boiling water

Sift the flour and cocoa into a mixing bowl. Add the sugar and make a well (hole) in the middle. Break in the egg, then add vanilla, milk and melted butter. Beat well with a wooden spoon, then put it into a well-greased casserole dish. Mix the cocoa, brown sugar and instant coffee together and spread over the cake mixture, then pour the boiling water evenly over the top (this settles under the cake mixture and becomes a sauce). Bake in a moderate oven for about 1 hour. Serve with ice cream or softly whipped cream and chopped nuts. Serves 5-6.

EDITH'S ECONOMICAL PUDDING

A comforting family style pudding for cold wintery evenings. As it cooks, a crumbly, moist sultana cake rises to the top leaving a caramel sauce underneath.

60 g (2 oz) butter or cooking margarine
⅓ cup sugar
1 egg
½ cup milk
grated rind of 1 lemon
1½ cups SR flour
1 cup sultanas

CARAMEL SAUCE
¾ cup lightly packed brown sugar
1 level tablespoon golden syrup
1 cup water
60 g (2 oz) butter
juice of ½ lemon

Put butter, sugar, egg, milk, lemon rind and flour into a basin. Beat with a wooden spoon for a minute or so. Mix in sultanas then put into a greased casserole dish. Put sugar, golden syrup, water and butter into a saucepan and stir over a medium heat to dissolve the sugar, then boil for 2-3 minutes. Add lemon juice, then pour syrup over the cake mixture. Bake in a moderate oven for 1 hour. Serve hot or cold with plain boiled custard (the recipe is on page 157). Serves 6.

CHRISTMAS IN THE KITCHEN

The house is decorated with Christmas bush and frangipani and a fat plum pudding hangs in an airy spot in the kitchen. The smell of the Christmas cake baking wafts through the house and mingles with the perfume of ripe mangoes and bright red plums. It's a curious mix of old and new, I agree, but I've always loved the special atmosphere of an Australian Christmas.

Christmas pudding, page 162.

CHRISTMAS PUDDING

*250 g (½ lb) each currants,
raisins and sultanas,
washed and dried
125 g (4 oz) pitted prunes,
finely chopped
3 tablespoons overproof
rum or brandy
250 g (½ lb) butter
1 cup brown sugar, lightly
packed
grated rind of 1 orange and
1 lemon
5 eggs
1 cup plain flour
½ level teaspoon
bicarbonate of soda
¼ level teaspoon ground
nutmeg
½ level teaspoon ground
cinnamon
125 g (4 oz) soft white or
wholegrain breadcrumbs (2
cups, firmly packed)
60g (2 oz) almonds, chopped
½ cup carrot, grated*

*To cook pudding:
2 litre (8 cups) pudding
basin or ¾ metre (30 in)
unbleached calico or 2 large
turkey sized oven bags*

Put dried fruit into a large bowl. Pour over rum or brandy,
mix well. Cover and stand for several hours or overnight.

Cream butter, brown sugar and citrus rinds until light and fluffy. Add eggs one at a time, beating well between each addition. Add sifted flour, soda and spices. Beat well. Add breadcrumbs, almonds and carrot. Stir in soaked fruits and any spirits left in bowl. Cover and stand for ½ hour to allow crumbs to swell. Stir (it's traditional at this stage to ask each member of family to stir the pudding and make a wish). Empty mixture into a greased pudding basin or tie in a pudding cloth (see deails following). Lower into **boiling water**. Cover and keep boiling gently for 5-6 hours (or 3 hours for 2 small puddings).

To reheat on Christmas day, lower puddings into boiling water and boil in a covered pot for a further hour. Serve with brandy sauce, hard sauce, custard or ice cream.

COOKING PUDDING IN A CLOTH

Scald pudding cloth in boiling water, wring out tightly. Spread out flat on a bench and sprinkle lightly with flour. Place cloth in colander or basin then pile in the pudding mixture. Gather material together at the top and tie with string (do not leave too much room for pudding to swell, as this often lets water in). Loop leftover ends and dust pudding with flour. Lower into *boiling* water and cover to keep in steam. When replacing extra boiling water, avoid pouring directly onto pudding. Remove cooked pudding by loop of string and hang in an airy spot to dry. Store puddings in refrigerator to prevent mould forming.

Note: Remove pudding from water immediately it is cooked.

IN A BASIN

Grease basin well with butter, then place a small circle of greased paper in bottom. This solves the problem of sticking when turning out on the day. Add mixture, cover with a circle of greaseproof or gladbake buttered on both sides. Cover with scalded and well wrung out pudding cloth or two sheets of foil. Tie with string. An additional handle made from double thickness string makes the basin easy to remove.

PUDDING CLOTH

Cut ¾ metre (30 in) unbleached calico roughly into a circle. Rinse in clear water to remove any dressing from the calico. Scald and wring out tightly just before wrapping the pudding (this swells the cloth giving a better seal).
If making double the mixture into a very large pudding, use 1 metre (39 in) of cloth.

OVEN BAGS

(These are a most successful way to cook miniature puddings and make great gifts). Split open a large turkey sized oven bag into a flat sheet (or use foil edged roasting wrap when available). Pile on sufficient mixture to tie up comfortably (using about 1-1.5 kg or 2-3 lb). Gather up into a fat round shape and tie with string. Tie loose ends into a loop. Boil in sufficient water to cover for at least 3 hours. A further hour when reheating on the day is needed. The basic recipe usually makes 2-3 small puddings.

HARD SAUCE

250 g (½ lb) unsalted butter
1½ cups icing sugar
mixture
1 teaspoon vanilla essence
2 tablespoons brandy, rum,
Cointreau or Kirsch

Cream butter with icing sugar in the small bowl of an electric mixer until light and fluffy (like whipped cream). Add vanilla and brandy, but just a few drops at a time because if added too quickly the butter could separate. Pile up into a small bowl or alternatively pipe into rosettes onto a flat baking tray lined with foil. Refrigerate until ready to serve. Enough for 16-20 serves.

BRANDY SAUCE

2 level tablespoons
cornflour
¼ cup sugar
2 cups milk
1 level tablespoon butter
¼ cup cream
½ teaspoon vanilla essence
pinch ground nutmeg
3 tablespoons brandy

Combine cornflour, sugar and some of the milk in a saucepan, smooth out any lumps with a wooden spoon, then gradually add remainder of milk. Bring to the boil stirring until thickened. Lower heat, cook a minute or so, then add butter, cream, vanilla and nutmeg. Remove from heat and stir in brandy, beat well.

HOUSE & GARDEN CHRISTMAS CAKE

This is the best fruit cake I know. The secret of success is to leave apricots and glace fruit in juicy little chunks so that the individual flavours are recognisable. So instead of a uniform flavour there's lots of delicious little surprises. It's a rich cake and very moist, but the whole character changes if overcooked so start testing after 2½ hours.

250 g (½ lb) currants (washed to remove any grit then spread out onto a tray to dry)
750 g (1½ lb) raisins
500 g (1 lb) sultanas
250 g (½ lb) each dried apricots, glace pineapple, dates and pitted prunes
125 g (¼ lb) each glace cherries and mixed peel
1 cup overproof rum (for economy use ½ cup brandy and ½ cup rum)
500 g (1 lb) butter
1 cup castor sugar
1 cup brown sugar, lightly packed
10 medium sized eggs
4 cups (500 g or 1 lb) plain flour
1 level teaspoon bicarbonate of soda
1 level teaspoon cinnamon
½ level teaspoon nutmeg
½ cup ground almonds
2 teaspoons glycerine (optional)
2 teaspoons parisienne essence (optional)
125 g (¼ lb) blanched almonds, chopped almonds halves, slivered or sliced, to decorate

2-3 tablespoons Grand
Marnier or Cointreau
brown paper and gladbake
or greaseproof paper to line
tins

Put currants, raisins and sultanas into a bowl. Chop
apricots, pineapple, dates, prunes, cherries and peel and
add to the bowl. Pour over the rum. Cover and stand
several hours or overnight.

Cream butter and sugars until light and fluffy. Add 8 eggs
one at a time, beating well after each addition. Add sifted
flour, soda, spices and ground almonds. Fold through
evenly. Stir in glycerine and parisienne essence (if used) and
all the fruit plus any rum left in the bowl and chopped
nuts. Mix well, then add the remaining 2 eggs and
thoroughly mix.

Prepare cake tins by lining them with two layers of brown
paper, then add an inner layer of gladbake or greaseproof.
This mixture will make one large 25 cm (10 in) cake or two
20cm (8 in) cakes. Put mixture into the prepared tin, spread
evenly and decorate with almonds (omit almonds if icing
the cake). Bake in a slow oven for 3½-4 hours for the large
cake and 2½ hours for the smaller cakes (reduce
temperature and cooking time if using a fan forced oven).
Start testing the cake after 2½ hours of cooking with a fine
skewer inserted through one of the surface cracks in the
cake. When cooked, remove from the oven and sprinkle
with the liqueur. Wrap in a clean tea towel and then in
several thicknesses of newspaper or a towel, so that the
cake cools slowly and retains the moisture. When cold
remove all the paper and put the cake into a plastic bag.
Try to leave for at least two weeks before cutting. It cuts
best after about 4 or 5 weeks.

Note: Glycerine absorbs moisture and this is used to make
the cake extra moist. It is available from chemists or
health food shops. Parisienne essense is simply used to
colour the cake a rich brown.

WHITE CHRISTMAS

2 cups Rice Bubbles
1 cup desiccated coconut
1 cup powdered milk
1 cup icing sugar mixture
½ cup each raisins and
glacé cherries, chopped
1 slice glace pineapple,
chopped
250 g (½ lb) copha, melted
2 teaspoons vanilla essence

Mix rice bubbles, coconut, powdered milk and icing sugar in a bowl, add the chopped fruits and mix through. Melt copha over a low heat and pour into mixture. Add the vanilla, mix well. Press into a foil lined lamington tin. Chill, then cut into squares. Store in refrigerator.

HAZELNUT SNOWBALLS

Sydney journalist, Gwenda Edwards, makes these dear little biscuits every Christmas to give away to friends. It is a lovely recipe and one of my special favourites.

250 g (½ lb) butter
1 teaspoon vanilla essence
½ cup icing sugar mixture
¾ cup hazelnuts, finely chopped
2 cups plain flour
additional icing sugar

Cream butter, vanilla and icing sugar. Add nuts and flour. Mix together into a dough, then roll into small balls in palms of hands. Place onto lightly greased baking trays

and press down lightly to flatten. Bake in a moderate oven for approximately 20 minutes. Remove from trays and cool, then store in an airtight container.
When ready to pack into airtight jars, toss biscuits lightly in icing sugar.

WALNUT KIPFERL

This is a personal favourite for Christmas baking.

125 g (4 oz) butter
¼ cup castor sugar
½ teaspoon vanilla essence
100 g can Diamond walnuts
1 cup plain flour plus 1 additional tablespoon (if necessary)
icing sugar mixture
1 vanilla bean

Cream butter, sugar and vanilla essence until light and fluffy. Put walnuts into food processor and process until finely chopped, making sure that they don't become oily by over chopping. Add to the creamed mixture with 1 cup flour. Mix into a dough, then take small pieces and roll between palms of hands. If the mixture is too sticky, add the extra flour. Form into little rolls tapered at the ends. Place on greased trays and shape into crescents. Bake in a moderate oven for 20-25 minutes. Overcooking spoils the flavour, so watch them carefully during last 5 minutes. Remove from oven.
When cold, place on a sheet of paper and sift over a light drift of icing sugar, turn over and repeat on the other side. Be careful not to use too much icing sugar as it can melt during the hot weather forming a sticky icing. Pack kipferl into a jar with the vanilla bean and seal tightly. Makes about 3 dozen.

ALMOND BREAD

Serve this crisp, wafer-thin almond bread with tea or coffee or hand around with drinks.

3 egg whites
½ cup castor sugar
1 cup plain flour
125 g (4 oz) whole almonds, unblanched

Beat egg whites until stiff, gradually add sugar in spoonfuls, beating until it reaches meringue consistency. Fold in sifted flour and, when mixed, stir through whole almonds. Put into a well greased bar tin. Spread out evenly into corners. Bake in a moderately slow oven for about 30-35 minutes (although pale in colour the bread will be sufficiently cooked when it starts to shrink slightly from the sides of tin). Cool, remove from tin and wrap in foil. Refrigerate for 24 hours.

Cut into wafer thin slices with a sharp knife or bread saw (an electric knife does a beautiful job). Freezing the bread for an hour or two also makes slicing easier. Set oven to lowest temperature. Place wafers on ungreased baking trays (usually three are needed) and dry out in the low oven for 30 minutes. Store in an airtight container.

Opposite: Almond bread, Walnut kipferl, page 169, Hazelnut snowballs and White Christmas, page 168.

HAZELNUT AND CHOCOLATE CAKES

These are little squares of hazelnut sponge cake with a baked-on chocolate topping. They are perfect to serve with after dinner coffee as they're not too sweet or rich.

1 level tablespoon fine dry crumbs to prepare cake tin
6 egg whites
¾ cup castor sugar
2 cups ground hazelnuts
2 level tablespoons plain flour

TOPPING

100 g (3½ oz) dark chocolate, chopped
1½ tablespoons water
¼ level teaspoon instant coffee powder
90 g (3 oz) butter
¼ cup castor sugar
3 egg yolks
1 teaspoon vanilla essence

Grease a lamington tin well with butter and sprinkle the dry crumbs evenly over the base. Whip egg whites until stiff, gradually add the sugar and beat into a soft meringue. Fold through hazelnuts and flour lightly. Put into prepared tin and spread evenly to corners. Bake in a moderate oven for 25-30 minutes.

While the hazelnut sponge is cooking, prepare the next layer. Melt chopped chocolate with water and instant coffee in a small saucepan over a very gentle heat. Cream butter and sugar. Add yolks, vanilla and melted chocolate mixture. When the hazelnut mixture feels cooked (slightly springy to fingertips and mixture starts to shrink from edges of tin), pour over the chocolate topping. Return to a moderate oven and bake a further 20 minutes. Remove from oven and cool in the tin. Makes 40.

MAUREEN DUVAL'S CHOCOLATE LOG

A good recipe for Christmas entertaining, this is a light chocolate sponge that's easy to make and not too rich.

5 eggs, separated
½ cup castor sugar
2 level tablespoons cornflour
2 level tablespoons cocoa
¾ cup thickened cream, chilled
1 teaspoon icing sugar
1 teaspoon rum or Cointreau

ICING
1 cup sifted icing sugar mixture
1 slightly rounded tablespoon cocoa
3 heaped teaspoons soft butter
few drops of vanilla essence
1 tablespoon boiling water

Line a Swiss roll tin with gladbake or greaseproof, making sure the corners fit. Brush well with melted butter (this is most important). Put egg yolks into the small bowl of an electric mixer and with mixer going at full speed, gradually add the sugar. Beat until thick. Sift cornflour and cocoa together onto a piece of paper, then add to egg mixture and blend well. Whip egg whites until stiff, then add chocolate mixture. Fold through gently. Empty into prepared tin, spread to the corners and bake in a hot oven for 10-15 minutes or until springy. Remove from oven and turn out onto a damp tea towel. Remove paper carefully (if it sticks, wet back of paper with a damp cloth). Roll up lightly folding into cloth, hold for a few seconds, then unroll and roll without teatowel. Cool. Whip cream until thick, adding icing sugar and rum, fill the cake, then ice. Chocolate icing: Beat together all ingredients.

GINGERBREAD MEN

125 g (4 oz) cooking
margarine
⅓ cup sugar
⅓ cup golden syrup
3 cups plain flour
½ level teaspoon ground
ginger
1 level teaspoon ground
cinnamon
3 level teaspoons
bicarbonate of soda (this is
correct)
1 egg
2 teaspoons vanilla essence

Put margarine, sugar and syrup into a saucepan and heat
gently, stirring occasionally. Cool to lukewarm. Meanwhile,
sift flour, ginger and cinnamon into a mixing bowl. Make a
well in the middle. Add the soda to the melted margarine in
the saucepan, then pour into the flour. Add egg and vanilla
and mix into a soft dough. Knead lightly with just a little
extra flour and roll out about 1 cm (just under ½ inch)
thick. Cut out with gingerbread man cutter. Bake on
lightly greased baking trays in a moderately slow oven for
10-15 minutes. When cool, ice all over with vanilla glacé
icing and decorate with silver cachous and red cherries.
Alternatively, if clever with icing pipes, decorate with royal
icing. Makes approximately 25.

Opposite: House & Garden Christmas cake, page 166.

GINGER CAKE

1 cup SR flour
1½ cups plain flour
1 level teaspoon
bicarbonate of soda
2 level teaspoons ground
ginger
½ level teaspoon ground
cinnamon
½ level teaspoon mixed
spice
¾ cup castor sugar
125 g (4 oz) butter or
cooking margarine
1 cup golden syrup
1 cup milk
2 large eggs
lemon icing

Line a lamington tin with gladbake, cutting corners to fit. Preheat oven to moderate. Sift flours, soda and spices into a large mixing bowl. Mix in sugar and make a well in the middle. Put butter and golden syrup into a small saucepan. Heat gently until butter melts, then pour into the dry ingredients in the bowl. Add milk and eggs and beat together well. Pour into prepared tin. Bake in a moderate oven for ¾-1 hour. Cool in the tin. Ice with lemon icing.

LEMON ICING

Place 1½ cups icing sugar mixture into a shallow dish. Add 2 heaped teaspoons butter, 1 tablespoon fresh lemon juice, ¼ teaspoon vanilla essence and 1-2 teaspoons boiling water. Beat well and spread over cake.

MINCE PIES

1 cup plain flour
1 cup SR flour
tiny pinch of salt
125 g (4 oz) butter
2 level tablespoons castor
sugar
1 small egg
1 heaped cup fruit mince

Sift flours and salt into a basin. Rub in butter and add sugar. Add egg and mix into a dough. Knead lightly with little extra flour. Roll out half the dough and cut out circles to fit shallow patty tins or individual tart cases. Fill with mince and glaze edges of pastry with water or egg white. Cover with small rounds made from the remaining dough. Make a steam hole in the centre of each one. Glaze with milk or egg white and bake in a moderate oven for 20-25 minutes. Store in a sealed container. Sift icing sugar over the top when ready to serve. Makes 1 dozen using patty tins or 1½ dozen if using the tiny French tart cases.

ICE CREAM CHRISTMAS PUDDING

An ice cream pudding with a surprise in every bite.

1 jar (275 g) seedless maraschino cherries
2 tablespoons Cherry marnier
1 tub (2 litres) vanilla icecream
100 g packet (3½ oz) round white marshmallows
1 violet crumble bar, chopped
200 g (7 oz) Vienna almonds, finely chopped
1 cherry ripe, chopped

Drain the cherries and reserve the liquid. Put cherries into a small bowl and add cherry marnier (don't be tempted to add too much liqueur as it will stop the ice cream freezing). Soak overnight. Next day, remove the ice cream from the freezer to soften. Cut marshmallows into quarters and add to the cherries. Transfer the ice cream into a large mixing bowl. Stir through all the remaining ingredients plus sufficient reserved cherry liquid to colour the ice cream a pretty pale pink (add few drops of pink colour if necessary). Put the mixture into a lamington tin and freeze until firm. Cover with two thicknesses of foil and store in freezer until Christmas day. Cut into squares. Serves 8.

AUSTRIAN JAM CRESCENTS

I am always amazed at just how well this easy pastry works. I discovered it in the 1950s when 'continental' cooking was enjoying a great deal of popularity in Australia.

125 g (4 oz) butter
125 g (4 oz) packet Philadelphia cream cheese
1 teaspoon vanilla essence
1 cup plain flour
raspberry or lingonberry jam
1 egg white
sugar

Put butter, cheese and vanilla essence together in small mixmaster bowl. Beat together, then mix in flour. Wrap in plastic and chill for ½ hour before rolling.

Roll out using a little extra flour, and cut into 10 cm (4 inch) squares. Spread with a thin layer of jam. Roll squares, starting from one corner, then form into crescent shapes on a greased baking tray. Brush with lightly beaten egg white and sprinkle with sugar. Bake in a moderate oven for about 25 minutes. Serve warm with coffee.

FONDANT ICING (PLASTIC ICING)

1 20 cm (8 inch) fruit cake
1 cake board, covered with
foil paper
2 rounded tablespoons
liquid glucose (maize syrup,
available from health food
stores)
1 kg (2 lb) pure icing sugar
2 egg whites
1 tablespoon glycerine
(optional)
1 teaspoon vanilla essense
or ½ teaspoon almond
essence
extra sifted icing sugar
melted jam or egg white (to
brush over cake)

Turn cake upside down onto a cake board so the surface to be iced is perfectly flat. Put glucose into a cup and heat gently in a pan of simmering water until softened. Sift icing sugar into a large bowl and make a well (hole) in the middle, then add egg whites, softened glucose, glycerine and vanilla. Gradually draw in about half of the icing sugar. Beat the mixture in the centre for a minute or so (this makes the icing very white). Work in the rest of the icing sugar making a pliable dough. Knead on the bench with extra icing sugar. Brush the cake with egg white or melted jam (so the icing sticks). Roll out the icing on a flat surface using a dusting of icing sugar on the bench and the rolling pin. Lift icing onto the cake with the aid of the rolling pin and smooth over quickly with hands. Cut off excess. Allow to set overnight before decorating.
A shell border of royal icing piped around the base adds a

finishing touch and helps to attach the cake to the board.
Note: A layer of almond paste could be placed on the cake
before covering with fondant icing.

ALMOND PASTE

4 cups pure icing sugar,
sifted
185 g (6 oz) ground almonds
2 tablespoons sweet sherry
1 tablespoon lemon juice
(strained)
2 teaspoons glycerine
2 egg yolks
extra pure icing sugar

Measure icing sugar and ground almonds into a mixing
bowl, then make a well (hole) in the middle. Combine the
sherry, lemon juice, glycerine and egg yolks and pour into
the well. Beat with a wooden spoon, gradually drawing in
the icing sugar until it becomes a stiff paste. Turn out of
the bowl onto the bench dusted with sifted icing sugar.
Knead lightly until it is a good consistency for rolling out.
If too crumbly, add a few more drops of lemon juice and if
too sticky add a little extra icing sugar. Cover tightly with
plastic until ready to use on the cake.
Almond paste is used as the first coating on a rich fruit
cake. This mixture is sufficient to cover a 20 cm (8 inch)
fruit cake. To cover the top only, make up half the recipe.

ROYAL ICING

1 egg white
1½ cups pure icing sugar,
sifted

Put the unbeaten egg white and icing sugar into the small bowl of an electric mixer. Beat at the lowest speed for approximately 3 minutes or until the icing is white and stiff enough to stand in soft peaks. Add a little more icing sugar if necessary.

To make by hand: Put egg white into a small bowl, gradually add icing sugar and beat with a wooden spoon or a flat wire whisk. Royal icing sets very quickly when exposed to the air so it must be kept tightly covered (with food plastic or a damp cloth) while using.

SOFT SNOW ICING

This is an easy icing to make for Christmas cakes.

125 g (4 oz) copha
4 cups sifted icing sugar
1 egg white
2 tablespoons boiling water
almond or vanilla essence
squeeze of lemon juice

Melt copha carefully (see packet instructions). Put into the small bowl of an electric mixer. Add 1 cup of icing sugar and beat well until thick. Add egg white, then gradually add the remaining icing sugar. Add the hot water a little at a time, then continue to beat until icing becomes creamy. Flavour with essence and lemon juice. Spread onto the cake and, using a spatula, swirl the icing into peaks to represent 'snow'.

COCONUT ICE

500 g (1 lb) icing sugar,
sifted
250 g (8 oz) desiccated
coconut
125 g (4 oz) copha
1 teaspoon vanilla essence
2 egg whites
pink colouring

Mixed sifted icing sugar and coconut together in a basin. Add melted copha and vanilla, mix well, then fold through stiffly beaten egg whites. Line a 20 cm (8 inch) square cake tin with foil or gladbake. Press half the mixture into the tin. Colour the remaining mixture a pretty pink and press evenly over the white mixture. Set in refrigerator, turn out and cut into squares with a sharp knife.

COUNTRY BAKING

Australian country cooks are the most wonderful cake-makers. Their enormously high sponge cakes filled with thick dairy cream and fresh fruit and their rich butter cakes are legendary. Some of those special recipes and many prize-winners at country shows are included in this chapter as well as the famous pumpkin scone and an easy recipe for bush damper.

Damper, page 186, and Shearers' scones, page 189.

DAMPER

The Australian damper or bush bread cooked in the dying ashes of the fire is the essence of simplicity. Here's a good recipe to make a light and crusty damper at home. The quick method of mixing with a knife is worth trying.

4 cups SR flour
2 level teaspoons salt
1 level tablespoon sugar
¾ cup milk
¾ cup water
beaten egg and milk to
glaze tops

Sift flour and salt into a basin. Mix in the sugar, then make a well in the centre. Pour in the milk and water and, using a knife, mix quickly into a dough. Do not knead or mix with hands. The mixture will be very light if simply emptied out onto a lightly greased scone tray and shaped roughly into a round loaf with plastic plate scraper. Glaze with beaten egg and milk. Bake in a hot oven for about 45 minutes or until golden. Serve in thick slices with butter and golden syrup and thick whipped cream. Accompany with scalding hot mugs of billy tea.

To cook in a traditional camp oven: Double the recipe and knead lightly with a little extra flour into a round shape. Grease the camp oven dish well, place in dough, rounded side up. Cut a deep cross in the top. Cover with the lid and bake in campfire ashes for approximately ½-¾ hour, depending on heat of the fire.

To cook on a bush picnic: Make up original recipe, divide into two and knead lightly. Shape each piece into a small French roll. Wrap in double thickness of foil, leaving room for the mixture to rise. Bury in the ashes for about 20 to 30 minutes, turning over once. Unwrap and cut into thick slices.

Twisties: Pinch off pieces of dough and shape into thin rolls with palms of hands. Spiral round thick pieces of green stick (make sure the stick used is a non-poisonous variety). Toast over ashes for about 10 minutes. When cooked, remove stick and fill the centre with golden syrup or jam.

CHEESE SAUCE SCONES

The melting cheese topping cooks to a beautiful golden brown.

4 cups SR flour
½ level teaspoon salt
90 g (3 oz) butter
2 teaspoons sugar
1 egg
1¼ cups milk

CHEESE SAUCE TOPPING

1 heaped tablespoon soft butter
1 cup mature cheddar cheese, grated
pinch of cayenne pepper
½ level teaspoon dry mustard

Sift flour and salt into a bowl. Rub in butter. Make a well in the middle of mixture, add sugar, egg and milk. Mix quickly into a soft dough, using little extra milk if necessary. Put dough onto a lightly floured surface and knead lightly with little extra SR flour. Pat out for thick scones (2.5 cm or 1 inch). Cut out with round scone cutter. Knead and re-roll scraps to use all mixture. Arrange close together on a greased baking tray or pack into a round shallow cake tin.

Combine ingredients for topping and spoon in little heaps on top of the scones. Bake in a hot oven for 20-30 minutes. Remove from oven, turn out onto a folded teatowel, and wrap loosely until ready to serve. Serve warm with soft butter.

To make herb scones: Add 2 level teaspoons dried mixed herbs to the flour before adding the egg and milk.

GEM SCONES

Remember these? They were my grandmother's speciality and now every time I make them it brings back happy memories.

60 g (2 oz) butter
4 level tablespoons sugar
1 egg
1½ cups SR flour
¾ cup milk
1 teaspoon vanilla essence
1 set gem irons

Turn the oven to very hot and place the gem irons in the oven to heat. Cream butter and sugar until light and fluffy, then beat in the egg. Fold through the flour alternately with milk and vanilla essence. Remove gem irons from oven and quickly grease with butter. Place mixture into gem irons (1 slightly heaped dessertspoon for each one). Bake in a hot oven for 10-15 minutes. Makes 24. Serve hot, split open and spread with butter. Delicious with a pot of freshly made tea.

PUMPKIN SCONES

A famous Queensland recipe!
For 1 cup mashed pumpkin, boil 250-375 g (½-¾ lb) trimmed pumpkin in a little water in covered pan for about 20 minutes. Drain well.

1 cup cooked pumpkin, cooled and well-drained
2 cups SR flour
½ level teaspoon salt
30 g (1 oz) butter
¼ cup castor sugar
1 egg
extra milk or egg yolk and milk for glazing

Mash pumpkin very well, drain away any liquid. Put flour and salt into a mixing bowl. Rub in butter, add sugar, pumpkin and egg. Mix into a dough. Knead lightly with little extra SR flour. Pat out dough to 2.5 cm (1 inch) thickness. Cut into about 12 small round scones. Place into a well greased 20 cm (8 inch) sandwich tin. Brush scones with milk or beaten yolk and milk and bake in a very hot oven for about 20 minutes. Remove from oven and wrap in a clean teatowel for a few minutes before buttering.

SHEARERS' SCONES

Serve warm with mugs of freshly brewed tea.

4 cups SR flour
½ level teaspoon ground nutmeg
½ level teaspoon salt
150 g (5 oz) butter
½ cup castor sugar
1 cup currants or chopped dates
1 egg
1 cup milk
beaten egg and milk to glaze tops

Sift flour, nutmeg and salt into a mixing bowl. Rub in butter. Mix in sugar and fruit. Make a well in the middle. Add egg and milk and mix quickly into a soft scone dough. Knead lightly using extra SR flour. Pat or roll out to about 2.5 cm (1 inch) thick. Cut out with medium sized round scone cutter (or a tumbler). Put onto a greased baking tray. Glaze tops with beaten egg and milk. Bake in a very hot oven for about 20 minutes. Empty onto a clean teatowel, cover loosely in a teatowel until ready to spread with butter. Makes about 16.

DATE LOAF

Serve cold, cut into thick slices and spread with butter.

1 cup dates, chopped
1 cup lightly packed brown
sugar
60 g (2 oz) butter
1 cup boiling water
1¾ cups SR flour
1 level teaspoon
bicarbonate of soda
2 teaspoons vanilla essence

Put the dates and sugar into a mixing bowl. Slice in butter (so it will melt quickly). Pour over the boiling water and stir until butter has melted. Add sifted flour and soda and beat well. Stir in vanilla essence. Bake in a well-greased loaf tin in a moderate oven for 45-50 minutes.

BANANA CAKE

A good banana cake is hard to come by, usually they're too soggy or too dry. This one is 'just right'.

125 g (4 oz) butter
¾ cup castor sugar
1 teaspoon vanilla essence
2 eggs
2 ripe bananas
1½ cups SR flour
¼ level teaspoon
bicarbonate of soda
¼ cup milk

Cream butter, sugar and vanilla. Beat in eggs one at a time. Mash bananas well with a fork, then beat into the creamed mixture. Fold in sifted flour and soda, then stir in milk. Place evenly into a well-greased 20 cm (8 inch) ring tin. Bake in a moderate oven for about 45 minutes. Remove from oven, cool for a few minutes before turning out onto a cake cooler. Serve sliced with whipped cream or ice with vanilla frosting.

VANILLA FROSTING

Mix 1 cup icing sugar mixture, 2 teaspoons butter, few drops lemon juice ½ teaspoon vanilla essence and few drops boiling water. Beat well.

ARMENIAN NUTMEG CAKE

This is an interesting cake to make.

1 cup plain flour
1 cup SR flour
125 g (4 oz) butter
2 cups brown sugar (lightly spooned into the cup)
1 level teaspoon bicarbonate of soda
1 cup milk
1 egg
1 level teaspoon grated nutmeg
½ cup walnuts, chopped

Sift flours into a mixing bowl. Rub in soft butter, then stir in brown sugar. Put half of this mixture into a well-greased lamington tin. Spread evenly and press down lightly. To the remaining mixture in the bowl, add the soda dissolved in milk, egg and nutmeg. Mix well, then pour over the crumb mixture in the tin. Sprinkle evenly with walnuts. Bake in a moderate oven for about 40 minutes. Serves 12.

CHOCOLATE ROLL

A chocolate cake made without flour was one of the amazing new ideas Dione Lucas introduced to Australia in the late fifties during her famous gourmet cooking demonstrations. There have been many variations on that famous recipe—this is my interpretation.

200 g (7 oz) dark cooking chocolate
⅓ cup water
1 level teaspoon instant coffee powder
7 eggs, separated
¾ cup castor sugar
300 ml (10 fl oz) carton thickened cream
1 tablespoon overproof rum (Cointreau or Grand Marnier could also be used)
1 rounded tablespoon icing sugar mixture
½ cup cocoa

Line a large Swiss roll tin or large shallow slab tin (see note below) with gladbake or greased paper, cutting corners to fit. Place chopped chocolate, instant coffee, and water in a thick saucepan, then stir over very low heat to melt. Separate eggs putting whites into a large mixing bowl and yolks into a smaller bowl (use an electric mixer if available). Whip yolks and sugar until thick and light then add chocolate. Whip whites until stiff. Pour in the egg/chocolate mixture, folding through quickly and lightly. Pour into prepared tin. Spread to corners. Bake in a moderate oven for 15 to 18 minutes. Turn oven off, wedge door slightly open with a tea towel and leave cake in the oven for a further ten minutes. Remove and cover with a damp cloth until cool.

Whip cream until thick, add icing sugar and rum. Remove damp cloth and sift cocoa evenly over the cake which is still in the tin. Loosen the cake at the edges and turn out onto a long piece of gladbake. Peel off paper lining. Spread cake evenly with cream and roll up loosely.

Do not be surprised if the cake cracks, that is usual and part of the character. Although the cake is very tender at this stage, after 24 hours of refrigeration it cuts perfectly and the flavour improves as well. Cut diagonally into thick slices and serve as a dessert cake with good strong coffee. Serves 12.

Note: A large shallow slab tin measuring 32cm $\times$ 27 cm (12½" $\times$ 10½") and 2.5 cm (1") deep is ideal for this recipe.

MUSHROOMS

Mushrooms were always the most popular thing at children's parties when I was growing up. They were my mother's speciality and she always made the best mushrooms. The tradition still lives on at our house, so whenever there's a party 'mushrooms' are on the menu. Here is her recipe.

1 recipe biscuit pastry (see page 194)
raspberry jam
1 recipe mock cream filling (see page 194)
cocoa
ground cinnamon

Roll out pastry between sheets of gladbake or plastic. Cut out with a 6 cm (2½ inch) round cutter. Line greased gem irons or shallow round based patty pans with pastry, trimming edges with a small knife. Put 1 scant teaspoon raspberry jam in each one and bake in a moderately hot oven for 15-20 minutes or until a pale golden brown. To make stems, roll pastry scraps between palms of hands into a few long, thin rolls. Bake on a greased tray 10 minutes. When ready to serve fill cooled jam tarts with the mock cream, dust over sieved cocoa and a little cinnamon. Add pieces of pastry to represent stems. Makes 20.

BISCUIT PASTRY

90 g (3 oz) butter or cooking margarine
½ teaspoon vanilla
3 level tablespoons castor sugar
1 egg yolk
1 tablespoon water
1 cup plain flour
½ cup SR flour

Cream butter, vanilla and sugar. Add yolk and water, then mix in sifted flours. Mix into a pastry dough, adding just a drop or two more water if necessary.

MOCK CREAM FILLING

2 level tablespoons cornflour
1 cup milk
60 g (2 oz) butter
2 level tablespoons castor sugar
½ teaspoon vanilla essence
few drops of pink colouring

Mix cornflour and milk until smooth in a small saucepan. Stir over medium heat until thick and smooth (like blanc mange).
Pour into a small mixing bowl, cover with plastic wrap so a skin doesn't form, then refrigerate until quite cold. Turn out onto a plate.
Cream butter and sugar until light and fluffy. Add 1 teaspoon of the blanc mange mixture and beat in well. Add remaining blanc mange *one teaspoon at a time* (not too quickly or it will curdle). Add vanilla and colour a pale pink. Store in refrigerator.

Opposite: Mushrooms, page 193.

AUSTRALIAN SPONGE CAKE

Australian country cooks are famous for their sponge cakes. Here's a prize-winning sponge cake recipe and tips for success.

4 eggs
¾ cup caster sugar
1 cup SR flour
1 level tablespoon cornflour
1 heaped teaspoon butter
dissolved in 4 tablespoons
boiling water
2 sponge sandwich tins
(20✕4 cm or 8✕1½ inch)

Grease cake tins with butter (add a tiny pinch of flour to butter to ensure a good crust). I always put a small circle of greased paper or gladbake in bottom of the tin as well to stop the sponge sticking in the centre. Whip eggs together with a rotary or electric beater for a few minutes until frothy (do not use a food processor as it doesn't give enough aeration). Sprinkle in the sugar, about 1 tablespoon at a time, and when all sugar has been added, continue to beat until the mixture is very thick (up to ten minutes*) Sift flour and cornflour together onto a piece of paper, then add *gradually* to eggs using a flat metal whisk (or use your hand). Stir through the hot water and butter quickly, then place into the prepared tins. Bake in a moderately hot oven for about 25 minutes. When ready the sponge will be springy to the fingertips and shrink slightly from sides of the tins. Remove from the oven and stand for a minute before turning out onto a cake cooler.

*A good way to tell when the eggs and sugar are beaten sufficiently is to firstly, turn beaters off, then dip a beater into the mixture then lift above the mixture and quickly draw a figure eight. If the impression holds for a few seconds, the mixture is ready for the flour.

Opposite: Australian sponge cake with passionfruit.

Note: Don't make the mistake of dumping in all the flour at once as this often results in little pockets of unmixed flour. Champion sponge-makers often bake this mixture in 2 deep 18 cm (7 inch) cake tins, resulting in a higher sponge.

IDEAS FOR DECORATING SPONGE CAKES

Passionfruit Sponge: Spread a single sponge cake with whipped cream (slightly sweetened and flavoured with vanilla essence). Drizzle over fresh passionfruit.

Strawberry Sponge: Spread a single sponge with whipped cream as above, then completely cover with halved strawberries, cut side down.

Iced Sponge: Sandwich two sponge cakes together with sweetened whipped cream. Ice top of cake with passionfruit icing.

Alternatively, split single layers through the middle, fill with cream, and ice one with Passionfruit and the other with chocolate icing sprinkled with coconut.

Passionfruit icing: Put 1 cup icing sugar mixture into a small shallow bowl. Add 1 heaped teaspoon soft butter and pulp 1 small passionfruit. Beat well. Add extra icing sugar if necessary. Spread over sponge immediately.

Chocolate glace icing: Sift 1 cup icing sugar mixture and 1½ level tablespoons cocoa into a shallow bowl. Add 2 heaped teaspoons soft butter and a few drops vanilla essence. Pour in 1 tablespoon boiling water and beat well. Spread immediately.

ORANGE BUTTER CAKE

A prize winner at many country shows.

125 g (4 oz) butter
¾ cup castor sugar
grated rind of 1 orange
2 eggs
1½ cups SR flour
¼ cup orange juice
¼ cup milk

ORANGE ICING
1 cup icing sugar mixture
1 heaped teaspoon soft butter
1 tablespoon orange juice

Grease a loaf tin well with butter and as a precaution against the cake sticking, line base of the tin with gladbake. Cream butter, sugar and grated orange rind until light and fluffy. Add eggs, one at a time, beating well after each one. Fold through sifted flour and, when thoroughly mixed, gently stir through the orange juice and milk. Place in prepared tin. Bake in a moderate oven for about 50 minutes. Test with a fine skewer before removing from oven. Stand for a few minutes before removing from tin. When cool, ice with orange icing made by beating icing sugar, butter and orange juice.

GINGER SPONGE

1½ cups SR flour
1½ level teaspoons ground
ginger
1 level teaspoon cinnamon
60 g (2 oz) butter, softened
to room temperature
½ cup castor sugar
2 eggs
½ cup golden syrup
½ cup milk
½ level teaspoon
bicarbonate of soda
2 tablespoons hot water
mock cream or whipped
cream
icing sugar

Grease two small sandwich tins (18 cm or 7 inch) with
butter. Line base of each tin with a circle of greased paper.
Sift flour, ginger, cinnamon into a mixing bowl (if using an
electric mixer, use small bowl). Add softened butter, sugar,
eggs, syrup and milk. Beat well with a wooden spoon or
electric mixer for a couple of minutes. Dissolve soda in
water and add to the mixture, stirring through very well to
blend smoothly.
Pour evenly into the prepared tins. Bake in a moderately
hot oven for about 25 minutes. Cool slightly before turning
out of tins. When cold, sandwich the cakes together with
mock cream or whipped cream and sieve a drift of icing
sugar over the top just before serving. Serves 8.

MOCK CREAM

90 g (3 oz) butter
4 level tablespoons sugar
4 tablespoons milk
½ teaspoon vanilla essence

Cream butter and sugar until light and fluffy. Add the milk *one teaspoon* at a time — if you add the milk too quickly the cream will curdle. By the time all the milk has been added, the sugar should be dissolved and the cream very smooth. Add vanilla.

CREAM PUFFS

CHOUX PASTRY

1 cup plain flour
1 cup water
1 teaspoon sugar
100 g (3 ½ oz) butter
4 small eggs (if using standard or large eggs, reduce to 3-3½ eggs)

Sift flour onto a sheet of greaseproof paper. Put water, sugar and butter into a saucepan. Heat until butter melts and as soon as water boils, add the flour. Beat well with a wooden spoon. Lower heat and cook mixture for a minute or so. Empty into a mixing bowl (use small bowl of electric mixer or a food processor). Break dough here and there so steam will escape and cool for a few minutes. Add the eggs, one at a time. Don't make the mistake of adding too much egg (see ingredients) because if the mixture is too thin the puffs will not rise so well.

Pipe or spoon onto lightly greased baking trays, leaving room to spread. Bake in a hot oven for 20-25 minutes. Remove from oven. Pierce puffs with a small knife and return to the oven for few extra minutes. Cool. Fill with sweetened whipped cream. Sift icing sugar over tops.

LAMINGTONS

Baron Lamington, who was Governor of Queensland during the later part of the last century, has often been credited as the inspiration for these cakes. However, according to Australian painter, Lloyd Rees, the Lamington was invented by a teacher of cookery at the Central Technical College, Brisbane—Miss Amy Schauer. Miss Schauer named these cakes, not after Baron Lamington (who was very popular at the time) but as a tribute to his wife, the Baroness.

1 butter cake or slab sponge (made the day before, see recipes following)
500 g (1 lb) packet icing sugar mixture
4 level tablespoons cocoa
½ cup boiling water
1 tablespoon butter
1 teaspoon vanilla
2 cups desiccated coconut

Place the cake in the refrigerator or freezer for about ½ hour or so before icing. Cut into squares. Sift icing sugar and cocoa together. Make into a smooth icing with boiling water, butter and vanilla. Pierce squares of cake with a fork and dip into chocolate icing for a few seconds, then toss into the coconut. If the icing becomes a little thick, heat over hot water or add a drop or two extra hot water to the icing. Lamingtons are best if allowed to mature in a sealed container for several hours before serving.

LAMINGTON BUTTER CAKE

—

125 g (4 oz) butter or cooking margarine
¾ cup castor sugar
1 teaspoon vanilla
2 eggs
2 cups SR flour
½ cup milk

Line a greased lamington tin with greaseproof paper. Cream butter, sugar and vanilla until light and fluffy. Beat in eggs, one at a time. Fold in flour and milk alternately and beat well. Spread into prepared tin. Bake in a moderate oven for 30-35 minutes. Allow to stand for a few minutes, then turn out onto a cooler.

LAMINGTON SPONGE

3 eggs, separated
½ cup castor sugar
1 cup SR flour
1 level tablespoon cornflour
1 teaspoon butter
3 tablespoons boiling water

Line a lamington tin with greaseproof paper. Beat egg whites until stiff, then gradually beat in sugar. Fold in yolks, then add sifted flour and cornflour. Dissolve butter in boiling water and fold through. Pour into the prepared tin and bake in a moderate oven for 20 minutes. Allow to stand for a few minutes, then turn out onto a cooler.

Note: A Lamington tin measures 28×20 cm (11×8 inches) and 3 cm (1½ inches) deep.

CARROT CAKE

Almost a meal in every slice, this cake is chunky and moist with cream cheese icing on the top.

⅔ cup raw sugar
1 cup sunflower oil
3 eggs
1 teaspoon vanilla
1 cup wholemeal plain flour
½ cup SR flour
1 level teaspoon each ground ginger, cinnamon and bicarbonate of soda
¾ cup walnuts, chopped
2 cups carrot, coarsely grated
½ cup raisins
450 g (14 oz) can Golden Circle crushed pineapple (very well drained)
2 level tablespoons coconut

CREAM CHEESE ICING
30 g (1 oz) butter
30 g (1 oz) Philadelphia cream cheese
½ teaspoon vanilla essence
½ teaspoon lemon juice
1 cup icing sugar mixture
nutmeg or cinnamon

Place in a mixing bowl raw sugar, oil, unbeaten eggs and vanilla, then sift in the flours, spices and soda. Add nuts, grated carrot, raisins, drained pineapple and coconut. Stir enough to combine ingredients, but do not beat. Line the base of a well greased 20 cm (8 inch) square tin with greased paper. Pour in cake mixture and bake in a moderate oven for 1 hour. Stand for 5-10 minutes before turning out. Ice when cold.

Cream cheese icing: Beat butter and cheese together then add remaining ingredients, adding a little more icing sugar if necessary. Spread onto cake and sprinkle lightly with nutmeg or cinnamon.

TREACLE TART

PASTRY
1 cup flour (half plain and half SR)
75 g (2½ oz) butter
tiny squeeze of lemon juice
1 tablespoon water

FILLING
½ cup golden syrup
grated rind of 1 lemon
1 tablespoon lemon juice
1 cup fresh white breadcrumbs
½ level teaspoon ground ginger
1 egg

Make pastry in the usual way then roll out and line a 18 cm (7 in) tart plate. Allow the pastry to rest while you make the filling. Combine all ingredients for filling and pour into pastry case. Spread evenly, then bake in a hot oven for 15 minutes. Reduce oven to moderate and cook a further 15 minutes or until filling is firm to the touch. Serve warm with softly whipped cream. Serves 6.

GRAMMA PIE

*An old favourite with
country cooks, Gramma
Pie is distinctly
Australian and really
quite different from the
American Pumpkin Pie.
The art of making a good
Gramma Pie is to drain
the gramma well,
extracting as much of the
liquid as possible. You
may have to ask the
greengrocer to order
it for you. It is
available during
autumn.*

**1 kg (2 lb) gramma (this is
trimmed weight, buy
slightly more)
⅓ cup sugar
juice and grated rind of 1
large lemon
grated rind of 1 orange
1 tablespoon sultanas
1 teaspoon golden syrup
1 level teaspoon mixed spice
or mixture of nutmeg,
cinnamon and ground
cloves**

**SPECIAL PIE PASTRY
1 cup plain flour
1 cup SR flour
pinch of salt
150 g (5 oz) butter or
cooking margarine
1 small egg
2 level tablespoons castor
sugar**

Peel gramma, discard seeds then chop into pieces and cook
with a little water in a covered saucepan for a good ¾ hour.
Drain in a colander until cold, pressing lightly to extract as
much of the liquid as possible. Transfer gramma into a
bowl, add sugar, orange rind, then juice and rind of the
lemon. Add sultanas, syrup and spice. Taste, adding more
lemon juice if preferred. Refrigerate until ready to make up.
Sift both flours with salt into a bowl, then rub in butter.
Beat the egg with sugar and add to flour. Mix quickly by
hand into a dough. Knead lightly with a little extra flour.

Roll out three-quarters of the pastry but not too thinly to fit a 20 cm (8 inch) metal pie plate. Fill with gramma. Wet edges and cover with remaining pastry, already rolled to fit as a lid. Press edges together with a fork to seal. Brush the top of the pie with milk or water and sprinkle with a little extra sugar. Bake in a moderate oven for approximately 1 hour. Serve slightly warm or cold with softly whipped cream. Serves 6-8.

ANZACS

The Anzac biscuit was introduced during the First World War as a tribute to 'the boys at the front'.

1 cup rolled oats
1 cup desiccated coconut
1 cup plain flour
¾ cup sugar
125 g (4 oz) cooking margarine or butter
1 level tablespoon golden syrup
1 level teaspoon bicarbonate of soda
3 tablespoons water

Put rolled oats, coconut, flour, sugar into a mixing bowl. Melt margarine and golden syrup together in a small saucepan over low heat. Mix soda with water in a small dish, add to margarine mixture and remove from heat. Pour into dry ingredients in the bowl. Mix well. Put onto well-greased baking trays in rounded teaspoons at least 5 cm (2 inches) apart as they spread. Bake in a moderately slow oven for 20 minutes. Makes 50. After removing from oven allow biscuits to firm up for a few minutes, then remove from trays with a metal spatula. When quite cold, store in an airtight container.

CHEESECAKE (BAKED)

*This is my favourite of all
the baked cheesecakes,
but please don't overcook
it or the centre will not be
so smooth and creamy.*

**1 biscuit crumb crust (see
page 210)**
**500 g (1 lb) Philadelphia
cream cheese**
½ cup castor sugar
3 eggs, separated
¼ cup plain flour
grated rind of 1 lemon
**1 to 2 tablespoons lemon
juice**
1 teaspoon vanilla essence
½ cup cream
**extra cream and grated
nutmeg for serving**

Beat cream cheese with sugar, add yolks and mix in well.
Sift in flour, combine well then add lemon rind and juice
and vanilla essence. Beat egg whites until stiff then whip
the cream. Fold these into cheese mixture. Spoon into
prepared crumb crust and bake in a slow oven for ¾-1 hour.
Do not overcook or the cheesecake may crack and the
creamy texture will be spoiled. Turn off the oven, wedge
door open slightly and leave the cheesecake in the oven for
a further hour. Refrigerate until quite cold. Release sides of
tin and serve cheesecake with additional whipped cream
and grated nutmeg. Serves 12.

CHEESECAKE (UNBAKED)

When cheesecake first hit Australia in the early 1950s, many of us were not quite ready for it and some found the baked cheesecake too 'rich' and heavy, so we developed a series of 'no bake' or 'refrigerator' style cheesecakes. This is a particularly good recipe and seems to appeal to younger palates even today when the cheesecake is very much part of the 'Australian Cuisine'.

1 cooked pastry case baked in a 23 cm (9 inch) spring form tin
4 egg yolks
1 cup castor sugar
grated rind and juice of 2 large lemons
½ cup fresh orange juice
2 sachets (1½ level tablespoons) gelatine
½ cup boiling water
500 g (1 lb) Philadelphia cream cheese
300 ml (10 fl.oz) container thickened cream, whipped
4 egg whites
1 teaspoon vanilla essence
fruit and whipped cream for serving

Put egg yolks, sugar, lemon rind and citrus juices together in a heatproof bowl (or in top half of a double boiler). Whisk over simmering water until frothy. Remove from heat. Whisk gelatine into very hot water (in a cup) and when clear pour into egg mixture. Beat cheese in the small bowl of an electric mixer, then gradually beat in warm egg mixture. Keep beating until smooth, then chill until just starting to thicken. Fold in whipped cream then last of all the stiffly beaten egg whites. Add vanilla essence and pour quickly into a spring form tin lined with cooked pastry. Chill overnight to ensure a good set. Release sides of tin and serve with fresh fruit (strawberries are particularly good with this cheesecake) and fresh cream. Serves 12.

PASTRY CASE FOR CHEESECAKE

Crumb crusts are fine if you're in a hurry, but I love the contrast of textures created by serving the smooth cheesecake in this crispy pastry case.

1 cup plain flour
½ cup SR flour
pinch of salt
100 g (3½ oz) butter
⅓ cup icing sugar mixture
1 small egg
1 oven bag and dried beans
(for baking 'blind')

Sift flours and salt into a basin. Rub in butter. Add icing sugar and egg and mix into a dough. Roll out (between sheets of plastic or gladbake) into a round large enough to fit a springform tin. Put pastry into the greased tin. Prick well. Split open the ovenbag and grease one side well with butter. Put the greased side to the pastry. Fill to the brim with dried beans and bake in a moderately hot oven for about 20 minutes. Carefully remove beans and oven bag and cook pastry 5-10 minutes longer to firm it up. Cool before using.

CRUMB CRUST

200 g (7 oz) Nice biscuits
90 g (3 oz) melted butter
1 heaped teaspoon castor sugar
¼ teaspoon nutmeg

Crush biscuits in a plastic bag with a rolling pin or use a food processor. Put into a mixing bowl and add melted butter, sugar and spice. Grease a 20 cm (8 inch) springform tin with butter.* Press crumb mixture firmly onto base and sides of tin (there is no need to take it right to the top as the cheesecake doesn't quite fill the tin). For a firmer crust, bake in a moderately slow oven for 10 minutes, cool and refrigerate before filling.

*When assembling the tin, turn the base upside down and cover with foil. Clip on sides of tin in usual way. This makes it much easier to slide the cheesecake from the base.

APRICOT NUT LOAF

This recipe is especially good and one of my personal favourites. Thanks to Australian House & Garden *magazine for permission to republish.*

1½ cups apricot nectar
1½ cups raisins
12 dried apricots, chopped
1 cup sugar
30 g (1 oz) butter
grated rind of 1 orange
1 egg
¼ cup milk
2½ cups plain flour
2 level teaspoons bicarbonate of soda
½ level teaspoon salt
½ cup walnuts, chopped
4 empty soup or juice cans (425 ml size)

Put apricot nectar, raisins, apricots, sugar, butter into a saucepan, bring to the boil, simmer for 5 minutes, then cool.

Add orange rind. Beat egg with milk, add to apricot mixture with sifted flour, salt and soda. When thoroughly mixed stir in walnuts. Place mixture into the four well-greased cans (no more than a little over half full because if too much mixture is used it will rise and overflow). Stand cans upright on an oven tray and bake in a moderate oven for 30-45 minutes. Test with a skewer. Cool for 5 minutes or so before carefully turning out of tins. Cut into thickish slices and serve spread with butter.

CINNAMON TEA CAKE

*60 g (2 oz) butter or cooking
margarine
4 level tablespoons castor
sugar
1 teaspoon vanilla essence
1 egg
1 cup SR flour
½ cup milk*

*TOPPING
soft butter
1 level tablespoon castor
sugar
1 level tablespoon
dessicated coconut
1 level teaspoon ground
cinnamon*

Cream butter, sugar and vanilla essence until light and
fluffy. Beat in the egg, then fold through the sifted flour
with milk. Place into a well-greased 18 cm (7 inch) sponge
sandwich tin. Spread mixture evenly. Bake in a hot oven for
about 25-30 minutes. Remove from oven and turn out onto
a cake cooler. Stand for a few minutes, then place onto a
serving plate and spread top of cake with softened butter
and sprinkle with mixture of sugar, coconut and cinnamon.
Serve warm or cold with a pot of freshly brewed tea.

APPLE TEA CAKE

Make up the tea cake mixture as above, omitting the
topping. Before baking, arrange tissue thin slices of
Granny Smith apple in a single layer to completely cover
the cake batter. Alternatively, use coarsely grated apple.

Dot with soft butter and sprinkle over 1 tablespoon brown sugar and sprinkle lightly with cinnamon. Bake for approximately ½ hour.

BILLY TEA

Hints for making a good brew.
- The first and most important thing is to have a black billy. This is simply an aluminium or tin billy, blackened by the fire. Why black? It heats faster, a shiny surface would reflect the heat.
- Place a green gum stick across the open-topped billy to stop too much smoke getting into the water. A lid of course would do the same thing (as well as making billy boil faster), but traditionally the billy was an old jam tin or 'bouilli beef can', hence the name.
- To stop the handle becoming to hot, always keep upright above the billy.
- When the water is boiling rapidly, throw in a handful of tea and remove from fire immediately.
- Now, this is the tricky bit: Hold the billy at arm's length and swing around in a complete circle. The purpose of this (apart from the theatrics) is to force the leaves to the bottom of the billy, leaving beautifully clear tea on top. For the faint-hearted, a few sharp taps on the side of the billy will do the same thing.

HOUSE & GARDEN CHOCOLATE CAKE

A moist velvety chocolate cake that always seems to work.

½ **cup cocoa**
½ **cup boiling water**
185 g (6 oz) **butter**
1½ **cups castor sugar**
3 **eggs**
2 **cups SR flour**
pinch of salt
¼ **level teaspoon bicarbonate of soda**
¾ **cup milk**
1 **tablespoon vanilla**

Blend cocoa and boiling water. Cool. Grease two 20 cm (8 inch) sandwich tins well with butter (add a tiny pinch of flour to the butter for a good crust on the cake). This cake is very tender so I always put a circle of gladbake in the bottom of each tin as well, just as an additional precaution. Cream butter and sugar until light and fluffy. Add eggs one at a time and beat in well. Sift flour, salt, soda and gently stir into creamed mixture, then add milk and vanilla. When well mixed, gradually stir in the cocoa mixture. The cake batter sometimes curdles at this stage, but don't worry, it won't spoil the finished cake. Pour into cake tins and bake in a moderate oven 30-35 minutes. Allow to stand for 5 minutes after removing from the oven before turning out.

The simplest way to serve this cake is to cut it into slices and top each piece with a spoonful of raspberry jam and whipped cream. To dress it up, fill with whipped cream and jam or well-drained sour cherries and ice all over with a Continental chocolate cream. Store the filled and iced cake in refrigerator.

Note: Alternatively, bake the cake in a 24 cm springform tin. For a finer texture, replace ½ cup of the SR flour with ½ cup plain flour.

PECAN ROLL

In this recipe fresh fruit and cream are rolled in a very light pecan sponge.

¾ cup pecans, finely chopped
3 large eggs, separated
½ cup castor sugar
¼ cup SR flour

FILLING
½ cup fresh berries (strawberries, raspberries or mixture of both), crushed and sweetened to taste
¾ cup cream, whipped

Line a Swiss roll tin with greaseproof paper, cutting the corners of paper to fit. Brush with melted butter and sprinkle with ¼ cup finely chopped pecans.
Whip the egg yolks with sugar until mixture is light and creamy. Gradually fold in stiffly beaten egg whites alternately with remaining ½ cup finely chopped pecans and sifted flour. Spread mixture into the prepared tin and bake in a moderate oven for 15 minutes or until cooked. (This mixture will not spring back so readily as an ordinary sponge, but it should not remain depressed when tested with finger tip.) Turn out onto a tea towel sprinkled well with sugar. Trim any crisp edges away with a sharp knife. Roll up and cool.
Stir the crushed and lightly sweetened berries into the cream. Unroll cake and spread with the cream mixture. Roll up and sprinkle with a light drift of icing sugar. Serves 6-7.
Note: Sydney food consultant and cookery writer Marie McDonald suggests that the pecans are best finely chopped with a sharp knife rather than a food processor for delicate mixtures. This cake is one of her specialities.

ROCK CAKES

Serve these fresh from the oven with a cup of tea.

2 cups SR flour
good pinch of salt
½ level teaspoon ground ginger or mixed spice
125 g (4 oz) cooking margarine
scant ½ cup castor sugar
grated rind of 1 lemon
½ cup sultanas or currants
1 egg
¼ cup milk
mixed peel

Sift flour, salt and spice into a mixing bowl. Rub in margarine. Add sugar, lemon rind and dried fruit. Make a well and add egg and milk. Mix quickly into a stiff dough. Place heaped dessertspoons of the mixture onto a greased baking tray. Put a piece of the peel on each one. Bake in a hot oven for about 20 minutes. Makes about 20.

PIKELETS

1 cup SR flour
pinch of salt
¼ level teaspoon bicarbonate of soda
2 level tablespoons sugar
1 teaspoon vinegar
½ cup milk
1 egg
½ teaspoon vanilla essence
1 tablespoon melted butter

Sift flour, salt and soda into a mixing bowl. Add sugar, make a well (hole) in the middle. Add vinegar to milk and pour into the flour. Add egg, vanilla and melted butter. Beat well until a smooth thickish batter. Heat a flat frying pan, electric frying pan or griddle and grease with a dot of butter. Drop dessertspoons of the batter (from tip of spoon for a perfect round shape) onto the pan and cook until the surface bubbles. Turn and lightly brown the other side. Remove to a folded cloth and cover until cool. Serve buttered.

GOOD SULTANA CAKE

375 g (12 oz) sultanas
½ cup water
½ cup sweet sherry
250 g (½ lb) butter or
cooking margarine
¾ cup castor sugar
grated rind of 1 large lemon
3 eggs
1 cup SR flour
1¼ cups plain flour
½ cup milk

Line a 20 cm (8 inch) fruit cake tin (6 cm or 2½ inches deep) with paper. Put sultanas, water and sherry into a heavy based saucepan and simmer gently until all the liquid has evaporated. Cool. Cream butter and sugar until fluffy, add lemon rind, then eggs, one at a time, beating well after each addition. Fold in sifted flours, then stir in milk and cooled sultanas. Place into the prepared cake tin and bake in a moderately slow oven for 1¼-1½ hours. Test with a fine skewer in the centre of the cake to make sure it's cooked before removing from oven.

SAVOURY BREAD ROLLS

Miniature bread rolls with a surprise filling of herbed onion.

1½ cups milk, scalded
30 g (1 oz) or 1½ level tablespoons fresh compressed yeast
4 cups plain flour (preferably bakers' flour)
3 level teaspoons salt
1½ level tablespoons sugar
¾ cup melted butter
1 egg yolk
extra ¼-½ cup flour for kneading
2 medium sized white onions, peeled and sliced or chopped
30 g (1 oz) butter
good pinch of dried thyme
6 or 7 fresh sage leaves, finely chopped (or ¼ teaspoon dried sage)
freshly cracked black pepper
good pinch of salt
1 egg white
sesame seeds

Cool the scalded milk to room temperature. Add yeast and stir to dissolve. Sift flour and salt into a mixing bowl. Add sugar, make a well (hole) in the middle. Pour in yeast mixture, then add melted butter and egg yolk. Stir into a fairly soft dough, then empty out onto a bench and knead using the extra flour. Return to a clean bowl greased well with butter. Cover and stand in a warm spot until well risen (about ¾-1 hour).

While bread is rising, prepare the onion filling.

Fry onions very slowly in the butter, taking about ½ hour so that the flavour develops and the onions are soft and glossy with just a tinge of golden. Add herbs and lots of freshly cracked black pepper and a good pinch of salt. Cool quickly in refrigerator.

Remove dough from bowl and knead lightly. Pinch off small pieces and flatten into little rounds. Place about ½ teaspoon of the onion filling in the centre then pinch dough together to enclose.

Put rounded side up onto a greased tray (close together so they cook in a batch). Cover with a cloth and rise for about 15 minutes. Brush with egg white and sprinkle with sesame seeds. Bake in a hot oven for about 20 minutes. Makes about 35.

If making the small, cocktail-size rolls, this mixture will make 50. The smaller rolls will take less cooking time. Serve warm.

These can be made ahead of time and stored in oven bags in the freezer. To reheat: Simply remove twist tie and place bag of buns in a baking dish. Heat and thaw in a moderately slow oven for about 20 minutes.

Serve warm with a chunk of cheese and salad. They are also good for barbecues. Miniature sized rolls are good to hand around at parties or with pre-dinner drinks.

WHAT WENT WRONG?

CURDLED WHIPPED CREAM

During the hot weather cream curdles very easily while whipping, and sometimes even when you are sure it wasn't overbeaten. Using thickened cream is usually safer as it is less likely to curdle. A good tip is to chill the bowl and beaters well in the refrigerator or freezer before you whip. *To save:* Providing it hasn't gone too far, stir a little extra unwhipped cream gently through and the cream should smooth out enough to be presentable.

PORK CRACKLING DIDN'T WORK

Take the rind from the pork and spread it out flat on a griller tray. Sprinkle with salt and slip under the griller for a few seconds (don't take your eyes off it as it burns easily).

WEEVILS IN THE FLOUR

If you discover weevils in the last packet of flour in the house while in the middle of baking, take heart in the fact that although aesthetically it is not too pleasant, the little weevil is not harmful to health – some even go so far to say that the food is biologically richer because the weevil has converted vegetable protein into animal protein. So simply sift them out and press on.

THE CAKE SANK IN THE MIDDLE

Cakes sink if they are not cooked sufficiently or if the mixture is too rich (too much butter or sugar for flour). If it is not too bad, turn it upside down and cover with cream or icing. Alternatively cut the centre out with a tumbler and turn it into a ring cake.

Rich fruit cakes that sink slightly can usually be saved as follows: When cooked, turn it out of the tin onto a flat baking tray. Place another flat tray on top and use weights. If the cake isn't badly sunken this treatment usually removes all traces of the mishap.

WATERY STEW OR CASSEROLE	Boil rapidly in a shallow pan until the juices are reduced and thickened. Alternatively, thicken with a beurre-manie made by creaming equal parts of butter and flour. This is then dropped in tiny pieces into the stew and stirred gently over heat until boiled and thickened.
STICKY FRIED RICE	When making fried rice boil rice the night before, or at least several hours before. Cook rice by which ever method you prefer (boiling salted water or by absorption) and spread out in a shallow tray. Cover lightly with plastic to stop too much drying out and store in the refrigerator. The oil should be hot before adding the cold rice and the heat kept high while frying.
CRUMB CRUST STUCK TO THE TIN	Biscuit crumb crusts often stick to the pie plate or springform tin. To prevent this happening it is always a good idea to heat the pie briefly over hot water (wrap a hot cloth around sides of springform tin). This melts the butter and helps to release the crust so that it cuts into neat slices.
BURNT CARROTS	Empty the carrots onto a chopping board by giving the pan a quick tap. Discard any badly burnt ones, trim the burn away from the rest and place them into a clean pan with a big dab of butter and a little sprinkle of brown sugar. Sprinkle in a pinch of dried tarragon and toss gently until glossy. Unlike most burnt vegetables, the smoky flavour with a touch of sweetness seems to work quite well with the carrots.
WHAT FLOUR IS THAT?	You have mixed up the canisters of flour and now you're not sure which is plain and which is self-raising. The best solution is to make a small batch of scones or dumplings, but if you are in a hurry that idea will probably not impress you too much. The next best thing is to use equal quantities of flour from each canister: that way you would have half the rising. For most cooking this wouldn't

221

be such a disaster as using *all* SR flour for a rich fruit cake or *all* plain flour for a steamed pudding.

Personally speaking, I think it's a good idea to always leave the SR flour in the packet, that way there is never any confusion.

THE TOFFEE CANDIED IN THE PAN

The easiest solution is to soak the pan and start afresh with a clean pan and fresh ingredients.

To make a perfect toffee: For every 1 cup sugar add ½ cup water. Put into a saucepan (not stainless steel) with a pinch of cream of tartar or a dash of vinegar or 1 teaspoon glucose. Stir over a moderate heat constantly until every grain has dissolved. Brush down the pan with a wet pastry brush to remove any stray crystals. The toffee should not boil until the sugar is dissolved.

Remove the spoon and boil rapidly (without stirring) until toffee starts to turn golden, then remove it immediately from the heat.

Toffee goes on cooking in the heat of the pan so it is wiser to undercook as it tends to burn easily.

BURNT TOFFEE

It's infuriating because it can happen so quickly. The only thing to do is to throw it out and start again. Here is a tip to save washing up. Take the pan from the heat immediately and *standing safely back* run the cold tap straight into the pan. The mixture will bubble but the toffee comes away from the pan in a flash. Please be careful though, as the resulting steam is very hot.

SOGGY CRUST UNDER FRUIT PIES AND QUICHES

That soggy almost 'raw' paste you find so often under quiches and apple pies is not pleasant to eat. Here is a tip that I have discovered to remedy the problem.

Put the cooked quiche or pie (still in the tin) over a very low heat on either a heat diffuser over a gas flame or on a flat scone tray on an electric top plate. The gentle heat from underneath dries out the pastry and makes it beautifully crisp.

THE CAKE STUCK TO THE TIN

This is annoying and so disappointing. Repair the damage while the cake is hot and hope it sticks together. Cover with icing or whipped cream. If it is too bad, turn it into a steamed pudding as follows: Heat up in microwave and serve with custard, or cool and crumble into a pudding basin, add a beaten egg and a few sultanas, cover and steam in a pan of boiling water for an hour. Turn out and serve with custard.

To prevent cakes sticking to the tin: Mix 1 heaped teaspoon of butter with ½ level teaspoon plain flour and use this to brush onto the cake tins. This gives a fine coating on the tins and most cakes rarely stick. A quick version of that same idea is to add a tiny pinch of flour to the butter when greasing the tins.

Some cakes are notorious for sticking and in that case it is safer to line the cake tins with a circle of greaseproof or gladbake.

ABOUT EGGS

Poaching: The white floated away in whispy threads leaving the yolks sitting there all alone! That happens if the eggs are stale.

Fresh eggs are the only ones to use for poaching. The white plumps around the yolk in a fat round when the eggs are only a few days old. Some people add vinegar to the water to strengthen the albumen in the egg, but I always think it spoils the flavour. A good pinch of salt will do the same thing.

How to tell if eggs are fresh: Break an egg into a saucer. If the yolk is in the centre and nicely curved and well banked up in a plump thick white with very little of the thin white around the outside edges, the egg is very fresh. As the egg stales, the yolks flatten and wander away from the centre and the white thins and becomes watery.

Red spots in eggs: This has nothing to do with quality, simply remove from the egg with small piece of shell before cooking. Incidentally, that little white, cord-like piece is not an embryo chicken as is sometimes thought, but is known as the chalazae which anchors the yolk in the egg and is usually more evident in fresh eggs.

223

Scrambled eggs: You have let them cook too much and they have lost their creamy texture. Simply stir in another egg or two, lightly beaten. The heat of the mixture will set the additional eggs and the mixture will be perfect.

Boiled eggs: How many times have you forgotten to time the boiled eggs for breakfast? Here's a tip to tell if they are just right for eating (whites set and yolks nice and runny). Remove an egg from boiling water with a slotted spoon and start counting. If on the count of 10 the water has evaporated and the egg shell is quite dry, the egg is ready. If not, return to the pot.

Broken yolks: There is no solution for broken yolks after the damage has been done, but if eggs are stored with the pointed end down the yolks are less likely to break.

While it may be attractive and have a country kitchen appearance to have eggs sitting in the kitchen in egg racks it is as well to know that eggs will lose as much freshness in three days at room temperature as they would in three weeks under refrigeration.

THE CURRY IS TOO THIN OR TOO HOT

Stir in coconut milk made by dissolving a little creamed coconut (available in small tubs in Asian shops and delicatessens). The coconut thickens the liquid and takes away some of the heat.

ABOUT GELATINE

The gelatine wouldn't dissolve: A problem many cooks have if they are not familiar with the use of gelatine. Here's how its done.

1. Sprinkle gelatine over cold water in a small dish, blending to a paste. Put this into a pan of simmering water until the solution is clear.

2. Pour hot (almost boiling) water into a cup. Assemble a fork and the measured gelatine. Gradually whisk the gelatine into the hot water and in a matter of seconds it should be completely dissolved.

3. Mix gelatine in cold water and heat in microwave for 45 seconds.

The jelly didn't set: Fresh pineapple and kiwi fruit contain an enzyme which prevents any gelatine dish setting. Always used cooked pineapple in jellies. I have found that kiwi fruit is not suitable for jellies, even when cooked.

Cloudy jelly: Some fruits such as quinces, loquats, some underripe fruits and sometimes grapes, often cause a jelly to cloud. While not harmful at all it does spoil the appearance.

Substituting leaf gelatine for granulated: Leaf gelatine is now available in Australia and it is handy to know the conversion.

The 10 g packets of leaf gelatine (usually contains six sheets) is roughly equal to 2 sachets granulated gelatine. 1 sheet leaf gelatine is equal to 1 level teaspoon granulated gelatine. The leaf gelatine may take a little longer to set with these quantities so increase slightly in a hurry.

WHY DID THE PAVLOVA WEEP?

This is a question often asked.

Some say the reason a pavlova weeps is that the eggs are weak or stale. Some say it is because too much sugar was used, while others say not enough sugar was used.

Too much vinegar is often blamed, but the most popular theory is that its caused by the weather! All these theories have merit.

The thing that works for me is placing the pavlova into a hot oven to start, then immediately turning it down to low. This initial burst of heat seems to seal the meringue quickly, giving it a crisp crust and the weeping rarely occurs. Sometimes there is a slight weep from underneath a corner of the meringue half way through the cooking which seems to dry out as the cooking time finishes. The addition of cornflour also helps and I have noticed that using wheaten cornflour gives a firmer meringue.

THE CAKE IS SMILING

Cakes crack if the oven is too hot. The reason is that the cake seals and then the uncooked mixture rises and breaks through the top surface. Loaf cakes almost always crack on top because of the shape of the tin. It never worries me if a cake cracks, but you can cook it at a lower temperature.

INDEX